INDIAN PRAIRIE PUBLIC LIBRARY DISTRICT

3 1946 00543 1850

OCT 3 1 2013

Curiosities Series

Kentucky
CURIOSITIES

Quirky characters,
roadside oddities &
other offbeat stuff

Third Edition

Vince Staten

D1159483

INDIAN PRAIRIE PUBLIC LIBRARY
401 Plainfield Rd.
Darien, IL 60561

Guilford, Connecticut

The prices, rates, and hours listed in this guidebook were confirmed at press time. We recommend, however, that you call establishments to obtain current information before traveling.

To buy books in quantity for corporate use or incentives, call **(800) 962–0973** or e-mail **premiums@GlobePequot.com.**

Copyright © 2003, 2007, 2013 by Morris Book Publishing, LLC

ALL RIGHTS RESERVED. No part of this book may be reproduced or transmitted in any form by any means, electronic or mechanical, including photocopying and recording, or by any information storage and retrieval system, except as may be expressly permitted in writing from the publisher. Requests for permission should be addressed to Globe Pequot Press, Attn: Rights and Permissions Department, PO Box 480, Guilford, CT 06437.

All photos by the author unless otherwise noted.

Maps by Alena Pearce © Morris Book Publishing, LLC
Project editor: Lauren Brancato
Text design: Bret Kerr
Layout artist: Casey Shain

ISSN 1932-7358

ISBN: 978-0-7627-6976-6

Printed in the United States of America

10 9 8 7 6 5 4 3 2 1

To Melanie.

She knows why.

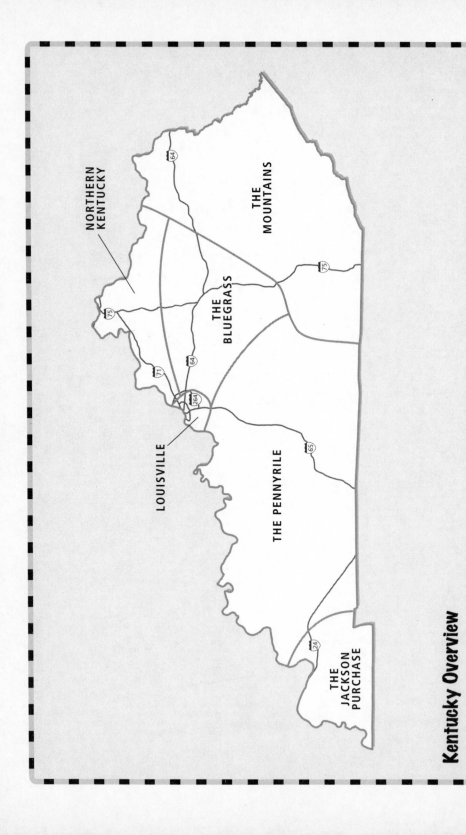

Kentucky Overview

contents

★ ★

acknowledgments

*F*irst and foremost I'm indebted to the people of Kentucky, past and present. This book wouldn't have been possible if Kentucky had been one of those boring states. This book also wouldn't have been possible without the generous help of the following people: my coauthor, Liz Baldi; my research assistant, Ashley Rae Needham; Jayne McClew of the Kentucky Department of Travel; Meta Marie Ball of the London-Laurel County Tourist Commission; Roy "Bud" Davis of Bert & Bud's Vintage Coffins; Bill Williams of the Louisville Slugger Museum; Bob Moody for Chicken Wolf; Tony Terry and Lane Gold at Churchill Downs; Jackie Jones of Hodgenville; Irma Raque of Kaelin's; Steve Vest and Mike Embry of *Kentucky Monthly* magazine; Jena Monahan of the *Courier-Journal;* David Jenkins, Laura Maraldo, Bruce Haney, Rod Irvin, Ronni Lundy, Larry Magnes, David Inman, Tom Jester, and Chris Wohlwend; my wife, Melanie Staten; my editor, Tracee Williams; and all the curious people of Kentucky (you know who you are).

And, finally, I recognize that a few towns will question their inclusion in a particular section. It was for geographic simplicity.

introduction

⭐ ⭐

How to Understand Us in Kentucky

When settlers from Virginia began pushing westward in the middle years of the eighteenth century, they hit a wall, literally. The Appalachian Mountains, which etched the boundary between Virginia and what would become Kentucky, seemed impenetrable.

But in 1775 a woodsman named Daniel Boone discovered the door through that wall—a gap in the mountains, the Cumberland Gap. You've probably heard about him and his discovery—it was in all the papers. When Boone and his band of thirty hearty souls crossed through that gap, they found a virgin land, completely unspoiled by human inhabitants. That was because not even the Indians would live there. Native Americans hunted on the land they called "Kentake" (an old Iroquois word meaning "the hunting grounds") and battled one another over hunting rights. But not a single Indian tribe claimed Kentucky as its home. It was just a nice place to visit and shoot deer. A lot of folks, particularly in the surrounding states, still feel that way. "Good place for hunting, but I wouldn't want to live there."

But soon many people *did* live there. The Cumberland Gap opened the way west, allowing pioneers from Virginia and North Carolina to rush into this uncharted territory and chart it. They pounded claiming stakes into the ground every hundred yards or so, laying claim to "this parcel of land that extends from the giant Oak ten steps from Grundy Creek to the tall Maple visible on the westward ridge" and to "that parcel of acreage beginning at Harmony Crossing and extending north to the fork of Owl Creek." Kentucky was soon a mishmash of competing land claims—so competing that when Kentucky was granted statehood a mere seventeen years later, in 1792, the deed map resembled a badly sewn quilt.

introduction

Kentucky's land deeds were a house of cards, a situation the US Supreme Court recognized when it ruled in an 1809 Kentucky land dispute titled *Bodley v. Taylor:* "The very extraordinary state of the land title in that country [Kentucky] has compelled its judges, in a series of decisions, to rear up an artificial pile from which no piece can be taken, by hands not intimately acquainted with the building, without endangering the structure and producing a mischief to those holding under it."

Not even the Supreme Court of the United States understood Kentucky. The justices just threw up their hands and said, "Fellers, you all know what you did. You work it out."

The land claim mess was what drove Kentucky's founder, Daniel Boone, to move on. At the end of his life, embittered over getting swindled in a number of land deals, Boone left Kentucky and moved to Missouri, where he died and was buried. Of course Kentuckians couldn't allow that. They stole over to the Show-Me State under cover of darkness, asked a resident to show them where old Dan'l was buried, and spirited his ashes back to Kentucky for a proper burial. But that's a whole 'nother story, told elsewhere in this book.

Folks, it's been pretty much the same ever since. Kentucky is a land unto itself. No one in the other forty-nine understands us, or needs to—except when traveling through and seeking directions. That's when we mess with your mind: "Okay, you know where the Gulf station is? No, well, how about the Mini-Market?"

Kentucky is a curiosity—a curiosity all its own.

One day a year Kentucky is the most famous state in the Union. That's Derby Day, the first Saturday in May, when the annual Kentucky Derby is run at Churchill Downs. On that day Kentucky is the home to fast horses, beautiful women, and great whiskey. For the other 364 days it is home to fast women, beautiful horses, and people recovering from too much whiskey. This duality—hey, we're important today, but tomorrow we're nothing—is a perfect reflection of a state of great curiosities.

Kentucky is the home of one of the most famous people in the world, Muhammad Ali. It is also the home of one of the most infamous, Charles Manson (his boyhood home is in Ashland—unmarked, of course).

America's first poet laureate, Robert Penn Warren, one of the most esteemed writers of the twentieth century, was a Kentuckian, as was gonzo journalist Hunter S. Thompson.

Illinois may have LAND OF LINCOLN on its license plates, but Kentucky was where Honest Abe was born. He just moved away rather quickly.

Curious, right? In fact, our license plate should say: KENTUCKY, LAND OF CURIOSITIES. It doesn't, of course. It says the BLUEGRASS STATE. And that's kind of curious itself. You see, bluegrass isn't blue.

These curiosities extend down to our counties: You can't buy a drink in Bourbon County (it's against the law to sell alcohol there), but you can in Christian County. Barren County is lush; Green County isn't.

The Jackson Purchase area of Kentucky wasn't purchased by President Jackson. He wasn't president in 1818 when the land was acquired from France. And while he did broker the deal, he didn't purchase the land.

Our state song, "My Old Kentucky Home," was written by a Pittsburgh native who may have visited the state—once.

Our most famous religious forefathers were the Shakers, who immigrated to Kentucky from New England. They were a religious sect that pretty much guaranteed their own demise by preaching celibacy. There are, as you might imagine, no Shakers left, just a ghost village that's been turned into a tourist site with a lot of nice solid Shaker furniture.

We Kentuckians pride ourselves on our high moral tone, meanwhile benefiting from an economy based on smoking (Lucky Strikes are made here), drinking (Makers Mark bourbon is distilled here), and gambling (Churchill Downs is situated here).

introduction

Our most famous export is Kentucky Fried Chicken, a fact that puzzles folks in Corbin, the hometown of Colonel Harland Sanders and home to his first restaurant. They are astonished that the world pays tribute—and lots of money—to their native son's fried chicken. They seldom ate the stuff. He was famous locally for his country ham.

Kentucky is famous for orators—from Henry Clay, the man who would rather be right than president and therefore was never president, to the two Cassius Clays, the nineteenth-century senator and the twentieth-century boxer. When asked what an orator is, Kentucky native and onetime US vice president Alben Barkley replied it was a man who when asked what two plus two is would respond, "When in the course of human events it becomes necessary to take the second numerical and superimpose it on the figure two, then I will tell you, and I say it without fear of successful contradiction, that the consequential results amount to four."

In Kentucky we do a lot of curious things: We Kentuckians spend $30,000 on a boat to catch a $10 fish. Our monthly satellite TV subscription fees run more than our mobile home mortgage payments. We collect broken major appliances on our front porches rather than send them to the dump. We erect concrete statues of Snow White and the Seven Dwarfs in our front yards.

I'd need an entire book to discuss all the curious Kentucky politicians, beginning with Kentucky native Abe Lincoln, who didn't carry the state in either of his presidential campaigns. Our politicians come by their, ahem, uniqueness honestly. What would you expect from a state where we still require politicians to swear in their oath of office that they have never fought in a duel?

We're proud of our curious history in Kentucky—so proud that we have erected 2,000 historical markers on roadsides around the state. Of course those markers don't tell you everything. For instance, Marker

x

★ ★

number 1869 tells the story of Henry Knox, the man who lent his name to the nearby fort where all the gold is. History records that Knox rode with President George Washington as he crossed the Delaware (you remember the painting). History did not record what Washington probably said to the three-hundred-pound Knox as he boarded the boat: "Shift that fat butt, Harry—but slowly, or you'll swamp the damned boat."

That's what this book is for: to fill in the small details that didn't make the markers and help you understand what a wonder—and wonderfully curious state—Kentucky is.

So how can you hope to understand us in Kentucky?

You can't. Just enjoy our curious ways.

Louisville

Wild Eggs

[60]
[265]
[64]

Wild Eggs
Kaden Tower

[264]
[42]
[60]
[71]
[150]

Louisville Ford
Assembly Plant

[265]
[65]
[160]
[264]
[60]

Ohio River

See Inset

0   3 mi.
0   3 km.

Inset:

Thomas Edison
Museum

Baxter Ave.

KFC YUM!
Center

Joe Ley
Antiques

Lynn's
Paradise
Cafe

[65]

Jeff Ruby's
Steakhouse

Muhammad
Ali Center

Ollie's
Trolley

Wagner's
Pharmacy

[150]

South 3rd St.

Louisville Slugger
Museum

Jefferson County
Courthouse

WAKY

Landmark Building

West Broadway

Seelbach Hotel

South 15th St.

Remains of
Louis Brandeis

West Oak St.

[31W]

0   1 mi.
0   1 km.

1

Louisville

Caution: Trick question *ahead.*

Do you pronounce the capital of Kentucky LOOEY-ville or LEWIS-ville?

The answer will determine if you need this book or not.

No, it's not LOOEY-ville. And it's not LEWIS-ville either.

One more guess?

No, it's not LOU-a-vull, even though that's how a lot of natives pronounce the name of the state's largest city.

It's pronounced FRANK-fort!

Louisville is not the capital; it's just the largest city, the most famous city, the most prosperous city, the home of the Kentucky Derby—and the city the rest of the state tends to dismiss as "not Kentucky."

To most in Kentucky, Louisville is a curiosity.

If you answered "Frankfort," then you may not need this book. You already know more about Kentucky than most non-Kentuckians.

★ ★

Batter Up!

It looms large—and strange—over Louisville's West Main Street: a gargantuan baseball bat. To the unknowing it might seem more than curious. After all, Louisville doesn't even have a major league baseball team.

But Louisville is home to the manufacturer of the most famous baseball bat, the bat that got its name from the town, the Louisville Slugger.

If you strike out using this bat, you'd better
consider a different profession.

This 120-foot-tall bat, standing at a jaunty angle, marks the entrance to the factory and museum.

Who could swing a bat this big? Not even Paul Bunyan could take a cut with this thirty-nine-ton stick. (The average major league bat weighs about two pounds!) It would take a man or woman at least twenty-four stories tall to wield the bat.

Inside the museum is the world's largest ball-and-glove sculpture, a seventeen-ton monument depicting a well-worn Louisville Slugger fielder's mitt holding a baseball.

Neither bat nor ball is authentic. The bat isn't ash but steel painted to look like wood. And the ball and glove were carved from a slab of 450-million-year-old Kentucky limestone.

The Louisville Slugger Museum is located at 800 West Main Street. For more information call (502) 585-5226 or check out the website at www.sluggermuseum.org.

Dog Day Afternoon

It's easy to bemoan the decline in nicknames. When the most famous basketball player of the modern era is nicknamed M. J. (Michael Jordan) and one of the most famous female singers is J. Lo (Jennifer Lopez), it's apparent we just aren't trying. Where are the imaginative nicknames? Back in the nineteenth century, baseball was loaded with players named Turkey (Turkey Mike Donlin) and Bow Wow (Bow Wow Arft) and Easter Egg Head (Easter Egg Head Shellenback).

There were some phenomenal nicknames for players back then (like Phenomenal Smith, a pitcher for the Phillies in 1890), but the most phenomenal nickname belonged to Jimmy Wolf. That's Jimmy "Chicken" Wolf, outfielder for the Louisville Eclipse in the 1880s.

Chicken Wolf led the American Association, then considered a major league, in batting average in 1890. But his greatest moment came on August 22, 1886. With Louisville and the Cincinnati Reds tied 3–3 in the bottom of the eleventh inning, Wolf laced a line drive toward the right field corner. The ball awakened a stray dog who had

3

been napping in the corner of the outfield, and the mutt joined Reds outfielder Abner Powell in a chase for the ball. When it appeared—to the dog anyway—that Powell was winning the race, the canine bit into Powell's leg and refused to let go. Wolf legged out an inside-the-park home run in what could literally be called the Dog Days of Summer.

In 1886 the Louisville Eclipse played their games in Eclipse Park, at the corner of Kentucky and Seventh Streets. Wolf is buried in Cave Hill Cemetery, 701 Baxter Avenue.

Mullet Central

You go for the corn dogs! You stay for the hair fashion—or out of fashion. For one week in late August, the Kentucky State Fair is the place to go to see mullets, beehives, big hair, and every other out-of-style style.

Ringling may have had the Greatest Show on Earth, but this is the Greatest Show in Kentucky. Position yourself on one of the benches on the Promenade and watch. They come from all over the state, folks who might never venture outside their home county the rest of the year, and they bring with them the greatest assortment of out-of-fashion hairstyles and haircuts.

Of course there's more to the state fair than corn dogs and bad haircuts. Head into the Main Pavilion and ask for directions to the Senior Citizen Center. Don't worry, we're not leading you to the quilting bee. Get the schedule for the annual Talking Contest. It usually attracts anywhere from a dozen to two dozen contestants. The rules are simple: The last man or woman standing and talking wins.

Each contestant is offered a chair. When the horn sounds, contestants are off and talking—and talking and talking and talking. One year the fair had to hand out four blue ribbons. After two hours there were four contestants who still wouldn't shut up.

The Kentucky State Fair is held the third week in August at the State Fairgrounds just off Interstate 65 on Phillips Lane. For more information call (502) 367-5002 or check out the website at www.kystate fair.org.

★ ★

Louisville Police Shoot Elvis!

When "The Pelvis" first performed in Kentucky on November 25, 1956, at the National Guard Armory, local police were so worried about riots that they filmed the entire show. In black and white. With no sound. Which seems to be against the point. Had they gone with color sound stock, a quarter century later they could have made a fortune selling the footage to David Wolper for his 1981 documentary *This Is Elvis.* Instead they got pennies for the black-and-white silent stuff.

But we're getting ahead of ourselves. What were they afraid of? That Elvis might incite teenage girls to—what? Scream? Faint? Chief of Police Henry Walker told the local newspaper his department was concerned that Elvis might incite a riot. In the end the concert went off without a hitch.

Other Elvis connections in Louisville: His grandfather, Jesse Presley, is buried here, in Plot 17 of Louisville Memorial Gardens. Jesse was Vernon's father and the estranged ex-husband of Minnie Mae Presley, who lived in Graceland and cooked many of Elvis's pan-grilled peanut-butter-and-banana sandwiches. He was also the namesake of Elvis's famous dead twin, Jesse Garon. Grandfather Jesse was in attendance at that 1956 show—the first time he had seen Elvis perform.

Elvis's first stalker also lived in Louisville. The King's FBI file contained a threatening postcard mailed from Louisville and records of threatening and harassing phone calls traced to a Louisville phone number. The caller would tell Elvis's family in Memphis that Elvis had been killed in a plane crash.

Elvis's "dangerous" 1956 show was at the National Guard Armory, now Louisville Gardens, a city-owned auditorium located on the corner of Sixth Street and Muhammad Ali Boulevard. Louisville Memorial Gardens is at 4400 Dixie Highway (US Highway 31 West), just south of Interstate 264. The phone calls were traced to a phone booth outside a Convenient Market at 3356 Broadway in downtown Louisville. Take the Broadway exit from Interstate 65, and head west for 3.2 miles.

Ten Rounds with the Quotable Muhammad Ali

1. "It's hard to be humble when you're as great as I am."
2. "It's just a job. Grass grows, birds fly, waves pound the sand. I just beat people up."
3. "I was the Elvis of boxing."
4. "I was so fast that I could get up, cross the room, turn off the light, and get back in bed before the light went off."
5. Before fighting Archie Moore in 1962: "Don't block the halls/And don't block the door/For y'all may go home/After round four."
6. "Howard Cosell was gonna be a boxer when he was a kid, only they couldn't find a mouthpiece big enough."
7. "Service to others is the rent you pay for your room here on earth."
8. "Prejudice comes from being in the dark; sunlight disinfects it."
9. "The man who views the world at fifty the same as he did at twenty has wasted thirty years of his life."
10. "The man who has no imagination has no wings."

Marvin Barnes's Time Machine

Marvin "Bad News" Barnes was the most free-spirited of the many free-spirited basketball players who passed through Louisville in the days of the old American Basketball Association. Marvin ate McDonald's hamburgers on the bench, paraded around the dressing room in a full-length mink coat with his uniform underneath, and accused his teammates of selfishness because they wouldn't pass him the ball when he had forty-eight points and needed only one basket to score fifty. In one season alone he missed more than one hundred team practices, but his most famous miss was a plane flight.

As Bob Costas, then team announcer for Barnes's team, the St. Louis Spirits, tells it in the book *Loose Balls:* "Because of the change of time zones, our return flight would leave Louisville at 8:00 a.m. and arrive in St. Louis at 7:57 a.m. Marvin looked at that and announced, 'I ain't goin' on no time machine. I ain't takin' no flight that takes me back in time.' "

You can't go back in time anymore, but you can travel at the speed of time. Southwest Airlines's schedule from Louisville to St. Louis lists most flights arriving ten minutes after their departure. But if you travel at 8:30 a.m., you can arrive in St. Louis at 8:30 a.m.

What would Marvin Barnes think of that?

Louisville International Airport is located at the intersection of Interstate 65 and Interstate 264. For more information check out the website at www.louintlairport.com.

Jefferson Never Slept Here

If people-watching at courthouses weren't interesting and unusual enough, the Louisville Courthouse has plenty of other attractions. At the front of the building stands a statue of the third president and principal author of the Declaration of Independence, Thomas Jefferson, who lent his name to this county. Why did he lend his name to the county? When Jefferson County was created in 1780 he was twenty years from being president. It was because he was governor of Virginia at the time and Jefferson County was one of three counties that were carved out of the mammoth Kentucky County, which in 1780 was still a part of Virginia.

Inside the courthouse rotunda is an engraved copy of the Jefferson's most famous contribution to American independence, the Declaration of Independence. Also on display in the rotunda is a marble statue of Kentucky hero and former Secretary of State Henry Clay. Though Clay

Jefferson turns his back on the courthouse.

was best known for his political career, he was also the father of five sons and six daughters. All six daughters and one son and his wife died before Clay from varying causes. Clay doesn't have much to do with Jefferson County. He lived in Lexington. But it is a nice statue.

The Jefferson County Courthouse is located at 700 West Jefferson Street.

The Remains of Louis Brandeis

Louis Brandeis was a brilliant scholar, perhaps our country's greatest legal mind. He graduated from Louisville's Male High School, which really was an all-male academy when he attended, in 1870, at age fourteen. He graduated Harvard Law at age twenty with what is reputed to be the highest grade average in the school's history.

One of his greatest accomplishments was the creation of what are now known as Brandeis briefs, a legal brief which relies on analysis of fact instead of theory. Believe it or not, before Brandeis legal briefs were all about theory. He was also instrumental in formulating the right to privacy via an article he coauthored for the *Harvard Law Review* in 1890.

He also served as an activist member of the Supreme Court from 1916 to 1939.

He died in 1941 and his cremated remains were buried under the portico of the school that now bears his name, the Louis D. Brandeis School of Law at the University of Louisville. It was the first time he had been back in Louisville in twenty years. He's been there ever since.

The remains of Louis Brandeis are located at 2301 South Third Street. For more information check out the website at www.law.louisville.edu.

Full Steam Ahead

There is only one rule in steamboat racing: There are no rules. So when the *Belle of Cincinnati* arrives at Louisville's waterfront each April to race the *Belle of Louisville,* anything goes.

The two tourist boats race from the downtown bridge to Twelve Mile Island and back, a race that usually consumes a couple of hours. It's not exactly thrill-a-minute action. But the revelers on the boats and on the shores don't notice. For them it's just an excuse to party.

The winner receives a set of mounted deer antlers, not much of an incentive for two hours' labor. But the antlers aren't the important thing;

Quintessential Kentuckians

Mike Barry—The Original Louisville Lip

They invented the word "ornery" for Mike Barry. Also the word "plucky." Barry, a longtime Louisville journalist and columnist, never met a community icon he couldn't kick in the shins.

Barry began his journalism career while still in his teens, writing a sports column for his father's paper, the *Kentucky Irish American.* He took over the paper in 1950 and did everything from writing front-page headlines to setting type. He loved the work but the pay, well, that was another matter. He had to take side jobs to keep his six children fed and clothed. He told the Kentucky Oral History Project, "At one time, I was doing the *Kentucky Irish American* every week, a weekly column for the *Louisville Times,* a daily radio show, being an odds maker for all the Kentucky tracks, and working the Kentucky Thoroughbred Breeders Association job."

He folded his newspaper in 1968 and became a full-time columnist for the *Louisville Times.* It was at the *Times* that he established his reputation for an acerbic wit. He was not a fan of the sportswriter as fan and went out of his way to chide writers who "fell in love" with

bragging rights are. The antlers seem to go back and forth, leading some local wags to suggest that all is not on the up-and-up.

Whether the Great Steamboat Race is the Ohio River's answer to professional wrestling hasn't been proved. But regardless of whether the fix is in or not, locals sure engage in some shenanigans to help the local favorite win.

the team they covered. "If you're a sportswriter, you never become a cheerleader," he said.

He also disliked the way local sportscasters referred to the Cincinnati Reds, located a hundred miles and a state away, as "our Reds." In his column he created the Reds Are My Second Choice fan club. "Anybody else is my first choice." He especially disliked the intense awe local sportswriters held for the beloved state basketball team, the University of Kentucky Wildcats, once writing that if Kentucky were to play the Russian National Team he wouldn't know whom to root for.

It wasn't just sportswriters who suffered from his withering remarks. His own editors were also targets. He once said of a Louisville newspaper big shot, "I think he ran away enough good men to staff four metropolitan papers."

Barry wrote about all sports but saved his greatest affection for horse racing. He was an inveterate bettor who claimed to have seen his first Kentucky Derby in 1922 at age twelve and to have missed the event only while serving overseas during World War II.

When he closed the *Irish American*, he donated the newspaper's files to the University of Louisville Library, which stored them in the rare book room. Barry claimed to be baffled, telling the Kentucky Oral History Project, "I thought a rare book was one that paid track odds."

Before 2009 the *Belle of Louisville* raced the *Delta Queen of Cincinnati*. One year as the two boats arrived neck and neck at the upper river turn, a pair of speedy tugs raced from the underbrush and helped the *Belle* make her turn, leaving the larger, heavier *Queen* to huff and puff to reverse course.

If you come, bring a stocked cooler.

There are numerous vantage points on both the Kentucky and Indiana sides of the river from which to watch, but the best viewpoint is on board. *Belle of Louisville* tickets invariably sell out. You can usually walk up and buy *Belle of Cincinnati* tickets at Waterfront Park, located at the foot of First Street on the Ohio River. For information on the *Belle of Louisville,* call (502) 574-2992 or visit www.belleoflouisville.org.

Bullets over Bullitt County

You can hear it long before you arrive: The sounds of *rat-a-tat-tat* and *kaboom* echo from the distant valley, a sign you are on the right road. It's the annual Bullitt County Machine Gun Shoot and Military Gun Show, and gun enthusiasts from both coasts arrive via motorcycle and RV for a chance to try out some of their heavy artillery.

You are liable to see just about any legal weapon, and a few that barely skirt the fringes of the law—not just rifles that would drop an elephant, but machine guns, infantry rifles, even bazookas. A serious shooter can go through a hundred-dollar ammunition clip in a heartbeat. And if you hang around long, you soon won't be able to hear your heartbeat.

Participants fire away at barrel drums, refrigerators, even old pickup trucks, reducing the targets to unrecognizable rubble.

This is, after all, the state that gave America Daniel Boone.

Bring your ear protectors.

The Bullitt County Machine Gun Shoot and Military Gun Show is held in early April and early October each year at the Knob Creek Gun Range, 690 Ritchey Lane, West Point, Kentucky, one mile off Dixie Highway on Highway 44. For more information call (502) 922-4457 or visit the website at www.knobcreekrange.com.

★ ★

Fireproof Blocks

It was the most technically advanced building in Louisville in its time, its time being 1855. It got the label because it was completely fire-proof! Still is. In a century and a half there's never been a fire. Why? Because everything from the heating system to foundation was designed to withstand a fire.

Before it was called the Landmark building, this enormous lime-stone structure was a post office, custom house, a newspaper office— the *Louisville Courier Journal*—even a home for the Chamber of Commerce. After a wide variety of owners, James and Kay Morrissey

No laughing matter: It's haunted.

bought the building in 1979 to house their local Weight Watchers program. While under the Morrissey's ownership, the building was placed on the National Register of Historic Places. It was sold in 1999 and renamed the Landmark building.

It's currently an office building. Oh, and it is also home to three friendly ghosts who are known among ghost hunters because of their incessant laughs.

What are they trying to tell us? That they aren't worried about a fire?

The Landmark building is located at 304 West Liberty Street.

Where Dr. Johnny Fever Got His Start

If you are a fan of the TV show *WKRP in Cincinnati,* you know who Dr. Johnny Fever is: the burned-out hippie deejay essayed by Howard Hesseman.

Dr. Fever had a real-life counterpart who got his start in Louisville radio: Skinny Bobby Harper.

Skinny Bobby was a legend at Louisville's WAKY, pronounced exactly as you would expect an early rock and roll station with the call letters W-A-K-Y to be pronounced, WACKY radio!

How wacky was WAKY and Dr. Johnny, er, Skinny Bobby Harper?

When WAKY switched from playing grandpa's favorite big band hits to playing rock and roll in 1958 it needed a way to drive away its older listeners and let young listeners know it was the new voice of rock and roll. To do that the station played "Purple People Eater" for twenty-four hours straight!

Honest. The disc jockeys would introduce other songs. "Okay folks, now here's a little Glenn Miller." But they would still play "Purple People Eater." Again and again and again, twenty times an hour.

It had the whole town in an uproar. According to an AP story, "The telephone people called (the station owner) and asked him to take the thing off the air. Too many people were swamping the switchboard. The police called, too. Listeners got the impression someone at the station had gone off his rocker."

Station owner Gordon McLendon explained his rationale to the AP. "People tune away to another station after so much of that, then they wonder if they're still doing that on that other station. So they turn back."

A number of well-known wacky deejays served time at WAKY in that era: Gary Burbank, who created and still voices the syndicated Earl Pitts; Skinny Bobby Harper, the aforementioned inspiration for the Dr. Johnny Fever character; and, perhaps the wildest of all, Jumpin' Jack Sanders.

Jumpin' Jack would swear on the air that he saw an alligator in the Ohio River. He would routinely sneak into the newsman's booth and set fire to the news copy while the announcer was reading it. His biggest stunt was bringing in Snake Man for a car dealership promotion. Snake Man would lie in a glass-topped casket, surrounded by fifty poisonous snakes. More than 40,000 people came out to see Snake Man. But not a single one bought a car.

WAKY's studios in 1958 were at 239 South Fifth Avenue. For more information check out www.79waky.com/printfeatures.htm.

And Down the Stretch They Come

The history of the Kentucky Derby is the history of great horses—Citation, Whirlaway, Secretariat. But it is also the history of some equine curiosities, including The Great Redeemer and Big Al's Express.

Redeemer was a big horse, only a half hand smaller than Secretariat, but he was more Clydesdale than sprinter, and he's the reason a horse now has to qualify. Redeemer had no business running against the best three-year-olds, but business was what got him in the Derby in 1979: His owner paid the entrance fee of $50,000, and Churchill Downs officials allowed him to be the twenty-third horse in the field. He broke slow and stayed slow. The traditional winner's photo was a wide angle shot: As Derby winner Spectacular Bid crossed the finish line, The Great Redeemer could be seen making the turn—a quarter mile behind in a mile-and-a-quarter race. Every five steps that Bid took, Redeemer fell one back.

Big Al's Express was a dream horse, the dream of California farmer Al Nesbitt, who had always dreamed of running a horse in the Kentucky Derby, even though he had no experience as a breeder or trainer. He bought a feisty Thoroughbred named Lucifer's Express, renamed him after himself, and headed cross country with the horse riding behind his old Buick in a single horse trailer. The Buick gave it up in St. Louis, but Al found a friendly soul who helped him get Express to the track.

Local sportswriters were waiting; they'd been hearing the Big Al saga for days from their counterparts on the path of the Buick. Big Al's Express looked good—shiny coat, attentive eyes. There was only one problem. He had never raced before. Officials told Nesbitt he could enter his horse in the 1983 Derby, but first the horse would have to

Witness the fastest two minutes in sports at the Derby.

★ ★

prove he could start from a gate. Three days later Big Al's Express was still shying away from a gate position. Finally Derby officials let Nesbitt run the horse from a standing start in a maiden race. To everyone's surprise Express took off, leading the field at the first turn. But it was not to be. The horse faded to last, dead last, forty-five lengths back, and Big Al and Big Al's Express reluctantly gave up their dream and headed back to California—in their Buick.

But it was a great dream, one seized on by many track regulars, who are but dreamers themselves.

Churchill Downs is located at 600 Central Avenue. Take exit 9, Southern Parkway, from Interstate 264 and follow the signs to the Downs. For more information call (502) 636-4400 or visit www .churchilldowns.com.

Hee-Haw Heaven

Yup, we got 'em. Or had 'em anyway. Big 'uns, too. Why the biggest 'un, Apollo, stood 19.1 hands high—which, for you city folk, is about six feet, six inches tall. That's at the rump. You don't measure mules like basketball players. His head was a whopper, too, measuring thirty-four inches long. Apollo and his buddy, Anak— mules are sterile, so there was no romantic interest there—were the two largest mules in the world according to the *Guinness Book of World Records.*

Apollo was born in 1977 and weighed in at 2,200 pounds. Anak, older by one year, weighed a hundred pounds shy of a ton and stood 18.3 hands high—a little over 6 feet tall. His head alone measured 32 inches long. Anak and Apollo went to mule heaven in 2001, just a few months apart. We sure miss 'em.

★ ★

The House the Colonel Built

It may sound like the food court at the mall but it's actually a basket-ball arena and the home of the University of Louisville basketball team. YUM! Brands Inc., which also owns such fast food royalty as Taco Bell and Pizza Hut, signed a $13 million, ten-year contract for naming rights. The logos for KFC, Taco Bell, and Pizza Hut can be seen by people flying over Louisville because with naming rights came the right to paint those logos on the roof of the stadium.

The arena's nickname is "the Bucket." Get it? The Bucket, as in a bucket of Kentucky Fried Chicken, I mean, a bucket of KFC. The company dropped the "fried" part of its name years ago.

Along with naming rights YUM! also got concession rights. There are seven concession stands throughout the stadium selling YUM! brands. So you can buy—pun alert—Honey Mustard Dunking Sauce or Apple and Cherry Turnovers or a Basket of Wings.

The Bucket, get it?

But no, your favorite player won't fowl out.

This complex has 22,000 seats, an Adidas store, the University of Louisville Hall of Honor, a sports bar, and a restaurant overlooking the Ohio River.

The KFC YUM! Center is located at 1 Arena Plaza. For more information check out the website at www.kfcyumcenter.com.

Almost Menlo Park

We coulda been a contender. Young Thomas Edison (he was nineteen) moved to Louisville in 1866 to work as a telegraph operator because the city was experiencing a shortage of such then. He settled in a small house in Butchertown, the meat-processing district, where he tinkered on plans for improvements to the telegraph. He didn't patent anything while living in Louisville, but he did spill acid on the floor of the Western Union office while experimenting on a new kind of battery. The acid leaked through the floorboard onto his desk, and he was fired the next day. He burned his desk in a rage, taking the next train northeast to Boston, where he would soon be issued a patent, the first of 125, for an electrical vote recorder.

We don't begrudge him leaving us and creating his scientific lab at Menlo Park in New Jersey. In fact we celebrate him with the annual Edison Birthday Celebration, held the first week in February at the Thomas Edison Museum, a tiny exhibition in his old house. The highlight is a display of light bulbs. There are also exhibits of proposed inventions from local elementary school students who hope to emulate Edison, at least in the inventing part—not in the leaving Louisville in a huff part.

The Thomas Edison Museum is located at 729–31 East Washington Street. From Interstate 64 take the Story Avenue exit (exit 8). Turn right at the first light onto Adams Street and follow Adams to East Washington. Turn right and go seven blocks. For more information call (502) 585-5247.

★ ★

More Fun Than a Barrel of Antiques

If you're in need of a ten-foot-tall toy soldier, you've come to the right place. Joe Ley Antiques has one. In fact Joe Ley has just about anything you could possibly use to decorate your home—and quite a bit

From monkey decor to mantels—
everything's for sale at Joe Ley's . . .

★ ★

that you couldn't. Architects and builders from all over flock to Joe's to peruse his more than 5,000 old doors; hundreds of mantels, balconies, and gates; and architectural ornaments of all shapes, sizes, and colors.

Joe Ley even has a category of merchandise the company calls "Monkey Decor." Want a monkey candleholder? Got it. Monkey cardholder? Got that, too. Even got a monkey sphere holder (a statue of a monkey on his back, holding a globe with his hands and feet; it'll set you back $20).

. . . except the cars parked outside.

Dr. Gonzo Born Here

The creator of "gonzo" journalism, Hunter S. Thompson, aka "The Doctor," hails from Louisville. Yes, the man known more for his hard lifestyle—heavy drinking, drug addictions, and being the first journalist to party like a rock star—was born and raised by his librarian mother in the Cherokee Park area. Oddly it was a story Thompson wrote about the Kentucky Derby that would catapult his career in journalism. Never mind that he made the entire thing up.

After graduating from Male High School, Thompson joined the Air Force in 1955 as an electronics expert. Although he had never written anything before, Thompson had always had an interest in books and writing, including serving as an officer of the Athenaeum Literary Association while at Male High. Not entirely interested in electronics, Thompson decided to try his hand at writing. He sent the editor of the Eglin Air Force Base paper, *Command Courier*, a story he wrote about the Kentucky Derby. He was hired as the sports editor, and the topic of the Derby would recur throughout Thompson's career.

Thompson grew tired of the Air Force and decided that he wanted to pursue a career in journalism. In October 1957 he received an honorable discharge and moved to New York City, where he took classes at Columbia University. Thompson soon got a job at *Time* as a copy boy and was delighted at his salary of fifty dollars a week.

Thompson's career took off, and in 1960 he began working in Puerto Rico for *El Sportivo*, a magazine dedicated to the sport of bowling, of all things. In 1967 Thompson published his first book,

Hell's Angels, about his experiences traveling with and being beaten up by members of the motorcycle gang. Two more publications brought Thompson into 1970. The first was an article that ran in *Scanlan's Monthly* called "The Kentucky Derby is Decadent and Depraved," where Thompson wrote, "Take my word for it folks, I have gone to the Kentucky Derby nine or ten times in a row, and I still have recurring nightmares about it that cause me to wake up sweating and screaming like some kind of pig being eaten alive by meat bats." The other coup for that year was the acclaimed narrative of his quest for the American Dream, *Fear and Loathing in Las Vegas,* which was made into a movie in the late 1990s starring Johnny Depp, another Kentucky native.

After this, Thompson focused on politics with *Fear and Loathing: On the Campaign Trail of '72.* His collection of ramblings, *The Great Shark Hunt,* explored Thompson's "distrust of anyone standing under red, white and blue bunting." In the mid-1970s Thompson took a turn on the other side of politics, running for sheriff of Aspen, Colorado. He lost—but garnered more media attention than any candidate.

Thompson took a mini-break from writing in the late 1980s. He was lured back by modern technology and wrote for ESPN.com, covering a variety of subjects, including—of course—the Kentucky Derby. He committed suicide in 2005. In a fitting finale Thompson's widow blasted his ashes from a cannon.

For more information on Hunter S. Thompson, visit the website www.gonzo.org.

★ ★

Just a Front

It may be true that a house is not a home. But when it comes to the Charles Heigold House in Louisville, it isn't even a house. It's just a front—a façade that has somehow managed to survive tornadoes and floods and even the wrecking ball.

It has one other claim to fame: It is also the only known monument to President James Buchanan. You remember President James Buchanan. Old Tippecanoe—no that was William Henry Harrison. *Old Ironsides*—no, that was a boat. Old Buck, that's it, that's what they called him. You do remember from junior high history that he was president, don't you?

And he has a monument, thanks to German immigrant Charles Heigold. Wanting to express his love for his new country and city, Heigold carved patriotic expressions into the front façade of his house. It just so happened that the rather boring Buchanan was president at the time. Not to worry, some of the nationalist sayings he carved include "Hail to Buchanan now and forever!" "All hail to city of Louisville!" "The Union forever, all hail to this Union, let us never dissolve it."

The house was originally located on Marion Street. Due to construction, however, the house was slated for the landfill until Mayor Charles Farnsley rescued the façade and had it relocated to Thurston Park on River Road.

Aside from being the only monument to Buchanan, the façade has received national acclaim. It has appeared in Liberty Bank commercials as a national symbol of patriotism.

The Charles Heigold House is on River Road, just west of Zorn Avenue.

James Buchanan put up a good front.

Row, Row, Row Your Boat

At its widest the Kentucky River is barely a hundred yards across. And the Ohio River, which forms Kentucky's northern border, is less than a mile across. That's why when Louisville native Tori Murden decided she wanted to row, she had to head to the east coast. Murden didn't have a little Sunday picnic in mind. She really wanted to row—across the Atlantic Ocean. And she did. In 1999 Murden became the first woman to row the Atlantic alone, an eighty-one-day trip that began in the Canary Islands off the coast of Africa and ended 3,333 miles later at Guadeloupe in the Caribbean.

Of course it was no average rowboat, not the kind you rent in the park. It was a sleek, high-tech model with global positioning equipment, a satellite dish, and a computer so Murden could file a diary on the Internet. How did she do it? "One stroke at a time, one step at time, the impossible is easy to achieve," she said upon her return to dry land.

Murden proposed to Mac McClure over her satellite phone while in the middle of the Atlantic, and the two married a month after her famous row. All together now: Sigggghhh.

National Farm Machinery Show and Tractor Pull

They come from all over: Big Sky cattle ranchers, Southwest sheep men, Carolina tobacco farmers, Northwest apple growers. Farmers of every stripe arrive in Louisville every February for the National Farm Machinery Show, the largest indoor farm show in the country. (Have you heard of any others?)

★ ★

They examine the latest in tractors, scrutinize advances in combines, kick the tires on mowers, and in general talk that back-fence talk that farmers swap when they meet on the back forty.

And then they go out on the town, too. Farm Machinery Show weekend is money in the bank for Louisville's restaurants and night-clubs. Restaurant owners grin ear-to-ear at the mention of the Farm Machinery Show. Some restaurants even have to import servers to keep up with the demand. Then the next morning it's up bright and early to *ooh* and *aah* over the latest in milking machines.

Did I mention that the farm wives stay back home and tend the farm?

The National Farm Machinery Show is held at the Kentucky Fair-grounds, exit 12 off Interstate 264. For more information call (502) 367-5004 or visit www.farmmachineryshow.org.

Old Rough and Ready

In the early 1990s a rumor—fueled by a newly published book, of course—swept through historical circles. Zachary Taylor had been poisoned. Yes, Old Rough and Ready, so nicknamed because of his slovenly appearance, had died only sixteen months after assuming the presidency. Had he been murdered with arsenic by his enemies, in particular, angry slave-owners? That in itself would be enough to get presidential historians up in arms, but there was a backstory. If Taylor had been poisoned, that meant Lincoln wasn't the first president to be assassinated—and that had Lincoln scholars up in arms.

There was only one solution—dig him up. The body of the former president was exhumed, after much teeth gnashing and public debate, and sure enough, he died of gastroenteritis, just like they always said. He'd been done in by a bowl of cherries and a glass of buttermilk.

They put him back in his grave in Zachary Taylor National Cemetery, 2109 Brownsboro Road. From Interstate 264 take exit 22, then turn west on US Highway 42. The graveyard—that's what we generally call cemeteries in Kentucky—is 0.5 miles down on the right.

Life isn't always a bowl of cherries.

Home of the Edsel

It is generally recognized as the ugliest car ever built, a guppy-faced monstrosity that makes even the AMC Gremlin seem merely homely. It is, of course, the Edsel, a Ford auto named for Henry's beloved only son, who died at age forty-nine in 1943.

Ford introduced the Edsel to an unsuspecting public in the fall of 1957. There was much fanfare, but the Edsel was met with a resounding silence. People whispered about that puckered-up grill and that ugly protuberance that ran along the side, an oblong boil some called the side trim. A few people bought them—a very few. After three production years, Ford mothballed its ugly little stepchild.

Today the Edsel is a collector's item, fetching thousands of dollars because of its rarity. But it's still an ugly, ugly car.

Every Edsel was manufactured at the Louisville Ford Assembly Plant on Fern Valley Road. Take the Fern Valley Road exit off Interstate 65 and head west. It's the big, ugly, industrial-looking plant.

Can't Stop Thinking about You

He's the original wise guy—sitting on his pedestal, pondering the fate of the world or the disaster that was his most recent blind date—or why his creator, the sculptor Auguste Rodin, didn't give him any clothes.

He is *The Thinker,* one of the most famous statues in the world. There are hundreds of copies in souvenir shops but only twenty-five original casts, and one of them is at the main entrance to the University of Louisville's campus. And this is the only cast made using the original "lost-wax" method, which dates to antiquity.

Rodin's original statue was a mere twenty-seven inches high. An over-life-size enlargement was created for a Paris exhibition. The first large bronze cast was not by the artist but by A. A. Hebrard in 1904 for the Louisiana Purchase Exposition in St. Louis. Rodin rejected it, and it ended up at the University of Louisville.

★ ★

The Thinker is in front of the university's administration building, Grawemeyer Hall. From Interstate 65, exit at Arthur Street; head west on Cardinal Boulevard, then south on Third Street a half block to the university entrance.

I think, therefore I am.

★ ★

Thunder over Louisville

You probably thought it was the Fourth of July fireworks at the Washington Monument—or maybe Disneyland. But the world's largest fireworks display is Thunder over Louisville, an annual street party that kicks off Louisville's Kentucky Derby Festival.

There was a time when the Kentucky Derby was the only attraction at Derby time. Then the city fathers added a parade, followed soon by a steamboat race, and pretty soon it was a weeklong festival. As more and more events piled up—bike runs, minimarathons, quilt festivals—it became Derby Week. It wasn't long till they couldn't contain all the celebrating in a seven-day period. That's when it became the Kentucky Derby Festival, a two-week celebration.

To kick it all off they introduced a giant fireworks show, held on the banks of the Ohio River, with a half-million dollars' worth of firecrackers going off over a half-hour period. It is spectacular, a sight worthy of comparisons to the opening ceremonies of the Olympics.

You want numbers? Try sixty tons of fireworks, 250 tons of launching tubes, two million pounds of sand to pack the firing tubes, seven hundred miles of wire cable connecting twenty firing boards, and 1,800 feet of barges to use for a firing platform. And they set it all to music.

Thunder over Louisville is held on the Saturday two weeks preceding the Kentucky Derby—which is the first Saturday in May—at the intersection of Interstate 65 and the Ohio River. For more information call the Kentucky Derby Festival at (502) 584-6383 or visit www.thunderoverlouisville.org. You'll probably have to park at least a mile away and walk to the riverfront—but, hey, it's free.

O. J. not O.K.

Long before O. J. Simpson was the man who was racing down a California Highway in a white SUV, he was a football star whose photo was on Jeff Ruby's Steakhouse wall in Louisville. However, after he was charged

★ ★

with murdering his wife and her friend and the nation watched his low-speed car chase, his picture was removed by Ruby. So when Simpson, who was in town for the Kentucky Derby, decided to stop in for a bite at Ruby's steakhouse, it was sure to be an interesting exchange.

The story goes that Ruby told Simpson, "I'm not serving you." Simpson and his party got their jackets and left the restaurant without causing a scene. As he exited, the rest of the restaurant applauded in support.

Jeff Ruby's Steakhouse is located at 325 West Main Street. For more information check out the website at www.jeffruby.com/louisville.php.

L is for Louisville

Mystery novelist Sue Grafton was born in Louisville on April 4, 1940. Grafton grew up down the street from fellow writer and Louisville native Hunter S. Thompson. When Grafton was in the third grade and Thompson in the sixth, he and his cousins use to "torture" her in front of Oti Forbse's Drugstore by riding their bikes along the back of her shoes as she walked by.

Grafton somehow made it out of the neighborhood and through the University of Louisville. She left Kentucky and moved to California in 1961, settling in Hollywood and working for fifteen years as a screenwriter. In 1982 she began her popular detective series with *A is for Alibi.* Her books have been translated into more than twenty-four languages.

Grafton decided to return to Kentucky after her book *L is for Lawless,* which takes the series heroine, Kinsey Millhone, to Louisville.

For more information on Sue Grafton, visit www.suegrafton.com.

★ ★

Where Tacky Is a Tradition

There are two kinds of tacky. There's the sad kind, where the host doesn't know that Velveeta isn't really an hors d'oeuvres cheese and that shag carpet is no longer cool. And there is the fun kind, where the host is playing along with the gag and everyone knows it's okay to laugh. Lynn's Paradise Cafe is the second kind: a fun establishment that's home to great food and great kitsch.

Bringing kitsch to a higher level.

★ ★

Take the table settings—not literally, of course, then Lynn's would be missing part of its personality. There are the adorable little salt-and-pepper shakers, the kind Grandma used to bring back from Florida and Mom would hide as soon as Grandma left. There are the hideous centerpiece lamps, the kind that Uncle Frank would send as anniversary presents. And there are the tables and chairs themselves, all retired dinette sets, rescued from a residence where the '50s never ended. Lots of chrome, lots of Formica, lots of Naugahyde—and lots of fun.

Plus lots of food. That's a Lynn's specialty: hardy portions that only a lumberjack could finish off. Like bacon and fried potatoes and heavy omelets. You'll win with Lynn. If you can only eat one thing, order the "Country Ham Eggstravaganza," a country ham steak and three eggs. You won't need to eat again all day.

Lynn's is also home of the Ugly Lamp Contest. What started as a goof—bring in the ugliest lamp in your house and win a free breakfast—is now an annual tradition.

Lynn's Paradise Cafe is located at 984 Barrett Avenue. From Interstate 264 take exit 16, Bardstown Road, north. Go left on Grinstead and right on Barrett. You can't miss it. There's a giant purple cow and a giant coffee cup out front. You can call (502) 583-3447 for reservations, but you don't really need them unless there's a bunch of you. For more information visit www.lynnsparadisecafe.com.

Eggs-cellent Breakfast

How does this sound for breakfast: Creamsicle Crepes?

Yummy, right? Especially if you have fond childhood memories of the orange-flavored ice cream treats. You just never expected someone to turn them into a breakfast item.

Well, Wild Eggs has.

Wild Eggs has reached the mountaintop of inventive breakfast fare with Creamsicle Crepes.

From the menu: "Warm crepes filled with sweetened cream cheese and orange marmalade, Grand Marnier Suzette Sauce, toasted macadamia nuts, fresh orange supremes, whipped cream, powdered sugar and cinnamon."

As delicious as it sounds.

Oh heck, even more delicious than it sounds.

And if you didn't grow up waiting for the Good Humor Man, there are plenty of other delightful wake-up treats, from Sweet Home Apple Bourbon Crepes to the Surfer Girl Omelet.

It's fun just reading the menu:

Batman and Reuben

The Frito Bandito Frittata

Leggo My Egg Roll

They even serve eggs! From Chicken Enchiladas and Eggs, "Chili" Verde Huevos Rancheros to Kalamity Katie's Border Benedict, Wild Mushroom and Roasted Garlic Scramble, and Mexico City Maria's Chilaquiles.

Don't just sit there reading this. Go order.

There are three Wild Eggs locations in Louisville: 3985 Dutchmans Lane, 1311 Herr Lane, and 153 English Station Road. For more information call (502) 585-5226 or check out the website at www.wild eggs.com.

Who Moved the Cheese?

If you're looking for the rat race, you've come to the right state. In Louisville there's the Run for the Roses, the nickname for the Kentucky Derby, and then there's the Running of the Rodents. It's a real rat race.

To coincide with the Kentucky Derby Festival—and to have a little fun—the students at Spalding University created the rodents race, which combines the competitive spirit of the Kentucky Derby with the academic regimen of biology lab, where white-coated professors run rats through the maze. Student-trained rodents go head-to-head against other student-trained rats in a two-lane maze. Winners move on in the competition. Losers go back to being lab rats.

It takes a couple of hours for the dozen or so rodents to make it to the final round, but when they do the brass band comes out and a crowd gathers to watch the Big Moment. We love a rat race, don't we?

Spalding University is at 833 South Third Street. From Interstate 65 take the Broadway exit. Head west on Broadway and then south on Third. There's no charge to watch the race. For more information contact Spalding University at (502) 585-9911, ext. 2405.

Hot Rod Redux

Science has created an expression for the phenomenon of pot-bellied men driving souped-up roadsters on main highways. It's called midlife crisis, and it's on full display every August at the National Street Rod Association's Annual Car Show held at the fairgrounds. These middle-aged men—and the participants are 99 percent male—take over the city's streets. You'd think you were back in the '50s from all the candy apple-red '55 Chevys and Ford Fairlanes with flame jobs painted on the side.

Mufflers that would get a high school kid a week's worth of detention are admired at this event, where more than 5,000 hot-rodders from across the country relive their adolescence for one weekend, competing in four categories and seven divisions. There's not a category for loudest muffler, but if there were, you can bet there'd be plenty of entries.

It's easy to find the Hot Rod Show. Just head to the intersection of Interstate 65 and Interstate 264, roll down your window, and listen for the revving sounds. The show is held the first weekend in August. For more information contact the NSRA office in Memphis, Tennessee, at (901) 452-4030.

Does Your Taffy Tolu Lose Its Flavor . . .

He called it Colgan's Taffy Tolu, and if that name had stuck we probably wouldn't be writing this capsule today. But, fortunately, wiser heads (and naming instincts) prevailed, and chewing gum entered the language and the culture.

In the years after the Civil War, Louisville pharmacist John Colgan noticed children peeling sticky sap from tree bark and chewing it. He knew there had to be a better way—tastier and more hygienic. So in 1879 he began experimenting, eventually turning to a medicinal gum called Myroxylon balsamum, which was used in ground-up form in a number of medicines.

Taffy Tolu had a strong, pungent flavor, but kids seemed to love it. Colgan began marketing the Taffy Tolu in a stick form, and it took off. In 1890 he sold his pharmacy and went into gum production full time. But the real watershed moment came when he sold Taffy Tolu at the 1893 Chicago World's Fair. It was a smash. A fairgoer named Wrigley noticed Colgan's success and began his own experiments, tests that led to Chicago and Wrigley Gum becoming the epicenter of chewing gum and poor John Colgan fading back into obscurity.

Soul Survivor

When the Seelbach Hotel opened its doors in 1905, owners Louis and Otto Seelbach had no idea that it would someday house notorious American gangsters, presidents, actors, celebrities, and even the living dead. A variety of ghosts are rumored to accompany the inhabitants of Seelbach.

One is said to be the ghost of twenty-four-year-old Patricia Wilson. In 1936, Wilson had moved to Louisville with her then husband. After four years of marriage, the couple separated. While trying to reconcile, the pair agreed to meet at the Seelbach. Her husband never made it. He was tragically killed in a car accident on the way to the hotel to meet with her. Wilson was overwhelmed and distraught by the news. Later, her body was found at the bottom of the hotel service elevator shaft. We still don't know if the fall was an accident or purposeful leap but we do know that since her death there have been multiple sightings of the grief-stricken woman. All sightings place Wilson in a blue dress with long black hair. Some even claim to have watched the ghost walk through the closed elevator doors or smell her perfume throughout the hallways.

The Seelbach Hotel is located at 500 South Fourth Street. For more information check out the website at www.seelbachhilton.com.

Horsin' Around at Wagner's

Once upon a time people ate breakfast and lunch at the drugstore. The days of the drugstore soda fountain are all but gone, except at Wagner's—where the burgers and shakes are almost as famous as the clientele. You can see famous horse trainers like Bob Baffert and Nick Zito eating breakfast, and famous jockeys like Shane Sellers and Pat Day having lunch. Everyone eats at Wagner's, even regular folks from the neighborhood. Wagner's just happens to be in an unusual neighborhood: It sits across the street from Churchill Downs.

The lunchtime crowd at Wagner's soda fountain is testament to the premise that if you have one, they will come. All of the seats are filled. One person slips out, another slips in—and the conversation never slows.

Every year at Kentucky Derby time TV network correspondents and newspaper columnists set up shop at Wagner's, broadcasting soda fountain scenes to millions all over the world—pictures of millionaire horse owners eating elbow-to-elbow with two-dollar bettors, of jockeys and trainers relaxing after an early morning workout.

Breakfast with champions.

Wagner's has been across from Churchill Downs for as long as anyone can remember. Owner Lee Wagner says his father started delivering there in 1910 and bought the place in 1922.

The hottest dish at Wagner's, literally and figuratively, is Kitty's chili, a signature dish created by soda fountain manager Kitty Wainscott, a woman who knows how to make her customers feel right at home.

"Kitty knows all the people," says Lee Wagner. "The Bafferts and the Zitos, when they are away from home, appreciate that."

Kitty closes the grill at 2:00 p.m. and only serves cold sandwiches till 3:00 p.m., when she shuts down and goes home.

Wagner's Pharmacy is at 3113 South Fourth Street, across from the track. Call (502) 375-3800.

Quintessential Kentuckians

Foster Brooks—the Lovable Lush

The most famous drunk in history is, of course, a Kentuckian. After all, this is where bourbon originated. Foster Brooks, the comedian known for his "Lovable Lush" character, became famous for staggering onto the set of TV's *Dean Martin Show*, slurring his words and coming within an ace of falling down. Martin was always entertained by Brooks's antics and kept him coming back week after week.

The irony of the Foster Brooks story is that Brooks didn't drink, at least not by the time he became the Lovable Lush. He'd been a bit of a rounder in his younger days, but in 1964 Brooks put down his martini and his cigarette and began leading a sober life.

Brooks grew up in Louisville, where his father was sheriff, his brother was a TV clown, and he was a child singer on the radio. He became a broadcaster, moving to Buffalo, New York, where he anchored radio news and teamed with Bob Schmitt—later Buffalo Bob Smith of *The Howdy Doody Show* fame—in a country music band. In 1960, at age forty-eight, he moved his family to Los Angeles to make it as an actor. It took a decade, but an impromptu speech at a celebrity golf tournament led to the creation of his Lovable Lush character. Tournament host Dennis James asked him to tell a few jokes. Brooks decided on the spur of the moment to tell them in his drunk dialect. And, thus, a legend was born.

★ ★

Nothing to Sneeze At

Technically it's the Kaden Tower. But everyone in Louisville calls it the Giant Tissue Box. And everyone in Louisville thinks it was designed by famed architect Frank Lloyd Wright.

Well, it does look like a giant tissue box. And it *does* look like one of Wright's offbeat designs. But it wasn't *quite* designed by Wright. Instead it was created by William Wesley Peters and Taliesin Architects. But there is a kernel of truth, since the blueprints were based on a design Wright created in the 1940s for a hotel in India. Wright's design was supposed to reflect Japanese influences, and when

Wrong about Wright.

★ ★

illuminated at night by the interior lights the building does resemble a Japanese lantern.

The tower was originally called the Lincoln Tower, for the Lincoln Income Life Insurance Company, the company that chose the building's design in 1965. In 1986 the building was renamed the Kaden Tower, a combination of the names of the new owners, Jim Karp and the Blieden family.

In a town full of glass box architecture, the pink building stands out as an oddity, whether you call it "the Pink Monstrosity" or "the Doily Building" or "the Giant Kleenex Box"—or just the Kaden Tower.

The tower is at 6100 Dutchmans Lane, just off Interstate 264, the Watterson Expressway, at the Breckinridge Lane exit (exit 18).

A Center Fit for The Greatest

Small museums usually have small visions. But the Muhammad Ali Center wants to be more than a repository of Muhammad's memorabilia. Its aim, as put forth in its mission statement, is to serve "as an international education and cultural center . . . a place to explore the greatness that lies within you and find the inspiration to pursue your potential."

Lofty goals indeed, but have you seen the building? It's no shack on the hillside outside a minor league ballpark, like the Dizzy Dean Museum in Jackson, Mississippi. It sits like a vision on the banks of the Ohio River, the waterway where Louisville native Ali once tossed his Olympic boxing gold medal to protest his hometown's racist attitudes.

The Muhammad Ali Center—or the MAC, as it is known—was designed by the renowned New York City firm of Beyer Blinder Belle. Pretty to look at, but also functional, the six-level, 96,000-square-foot MAC contains an auditorium, two galleries, an archive and library, and a two-level outdoor plaza that connects the building to the adjacent Kentucky Center for the Arts.

The MAC opened in November 2005 with a gala featuring Ali himself, a who's who of the sports and entertainment industries, and former president Bill Clinton.

It takes a day to view all the exhibits, and that doesn't include special programs like a photo gallery by well-known Ali photographer Howard Bingham.

The Muhammad Ali Center is at 144 North Sixth Street. Call (502) 584-9254 or visit www.alicenter.org.

Big MAC.

Kentucky, the License Plate State

Our plates read simply Bluegrass State, despite the fact that no one outside Kentucky has any idea what bluegrass is, much less that it isn't blue. We could put a lot of different slogans on our license plates, because Kentucky truly is the Land of Curiosities. Here are just a few:

The Post Office State—Kentucky has more post offices per capita than any other state.

If You Can Read This Bumper Sticker You Aren't from Kentucky—Kentucky has the lowest percentage of adults twenty-five and over without a high school diploma.

Greater Kentucky—Kentucky claims its border extends all the way to the Indiana shoreline of the Ohio River and has made threats to close down Indiana's casino boats.

The Game Show State—Famous game show hosts Jack Narz, Chuck Woolery, and Tom Kennedy are all from Kentucky.

Gateway to the Wild Wild West—Judge Roy Bean, Jim Bowie, and Kit Carson were all born in Kentucky.

The Governor State—More than a hundred native Kentuckians have been elected governors of other states.

The Volunteer State—They call Tennessee the Volunteer State, but in the War of 1812 more than half of all Americans killed in action were Kentuckians.

Incidentally, all our license plates are manufactured at the Kentucky State Reformatory in LaGrange. They cost about $1.45 each to make.

Clang, Clang, Clang Went the . . .

It was supposed to be the next Kentucky Fried Chicken. When John Y. Brown, one of the founders of the chicken chain, purchased Ollie's Trolley (Ollie's, for short) in 1973, his goal was to turn it into a national fast food sensation. But, alas—at least for Brown—McDonald's had conditioned the national taste buds to expect mustard and ketchup on its burgers, and Mr. Ollie would have none of that. The original Ollie Burger was a gourmet-sized burger, cooked rare, sprinkled with a concoction of twenty-three herbs and spices (Brown's original chicken partner, Harlan Sanders, had only eleven herbs and spices in his secret mix) and coated with a secret sauce.

Zing, zing, zing went the sauce.

The Ollie's gimmick was that all the restaurants were housed in red-and-yellow trolley-shaped buildings, meaning long lines at lunchtime. Most Ollie's went the way of the trolley, but a handful of the restaurants remain, including this one in downtown Louisville at the corner of Third and Kentucky.

Ollie's has adapted to the times (no more rare meat; mustard and ketchup are readily available), but it's still a gourmet treat—guaranteed to drip all over your upholstery, because the best way to eat it is on the spot, in your car (Ollie's has no seating except for a couple of picnic tables).

The secret is still the secret sauce, an elixir so good that the old Lum's chain used to offer Ollie Sauce with its hot dogs. Between you and me, it tastes a lot like Thousand Island dressing that's heavy on the mayo and spices.

Ollie's is located at 978 South Third Street in downtown Louisville. The phone number is (502) 583-5214.

2

The Bluegrass

How will you *know when you're in Kentucky's famous Bluegrass region? As soon as the grass turns blue, dummy. Actually that's not true. Bluegrass is not blue. It's—surprise!—green, just like every other kind of grass you've ever seen except dead grass, which is brown.*

No, you'll know you're in The Bluegrass when you start passing barns that are nicer than your house. That's because the inhabitants, Thoroughbred racehorses, are worth more than you are. A yearling can go at auction for as much as $4 million. That's a one-year-old horse! The Bluegrass region is responsible for Kentucky's reputation as the home of fast horses and beautiful women. Or is it fast women and beautiful horses?

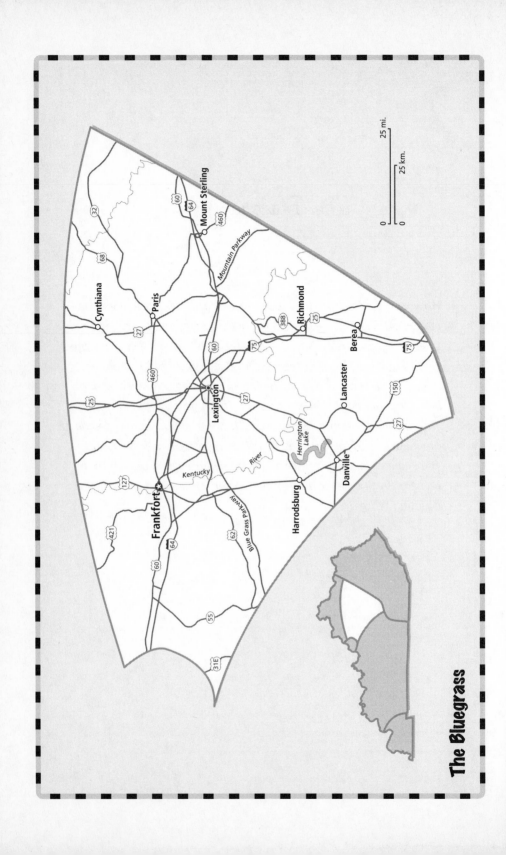

The Bluegrass

Just a Spoonful of . . . Bread?

Berea

Spoonbread is not quite cornbread, and actually not quite bread at all. It's, well, spoonbread. Since the early 1990s Berea has held an annual festival celebrating the odd concoction.

Spoonbread—a mushy, bread-like substance made from cornmeal—was made famous by Boone Tavern at Berea College. If you ask the locals to describe it, they'll tell you it's a "cornbread soufflé." (Don't tell them, but it still tastes like mush.)

The festival itself doesn't really celebrate the bread. Instead, it celebrates the fame the bread has brought the region. Drawing crowds of more than 10,000 each year, participants partake in a 5K run, hot air balloon displays, softball tournaments, and the crowning of Miss Berea—all the usual stuff you find at a small town festival, plus spoonbread. The Spoonbread Festival is held the Friday following Labor Day in Memorial Park.

For information call (859) 986-9760 or visit www.spoonbread festival.com.

Stuck on You

Cynthiana

There was a time, although it's hard to remember, without Post-it notes. The reason it's hard to remember is because I don't have a Post-it note to remind me!

Post-it notes, those yellow slips of paper with a sticky streak at one end, help keep the world organized. Have trouble remembering your doctor's appointments? Put a Post-it note on your computer. In fact, put up a Post-it note to help remember everything in your life.

Post-it notes have only been around since the 1970s. They were invented by a 3M Company scientist named Art Fry. The problem wasn't in making them stick; it was getting people to use them. 3M resorted to giving away the little yellow pads just to get people hooked. It worked.

And they're not just yellow squares anymore—they come in eight standard sizes, twenty-five shapes, and sixty-two colors.

If you thought you could escape the ubiquitous Post-it note by logging on to your computer, wrong; 3M also has computer Post-it notes. And Cynthiana is Post-it's home—all gazillion of them are manufactured right here.

3M's Post-it manufacturing plant is at 301 New Lair Road. Sorry, there are no tours. 3M doesn't want its secret technology getting into the wrong hands . . . and onto the wrong refrigerators . . . and computer monitors.

Bite This Bullet
Danville

You've heard the expression "bite the bullet." It usually means "get ready for an unpleasant task." But in the olden days, back when Betty White was a girl, it literally meant bite the bullet. Someone about to undergo a difficult surgery was given something to bite on to distract the brain from the intense pain. Usually it was a towel or a wooden spoon, but those didn't make for colorful story-telling. So pioneers returning from the Old West would tell tales of biting the bullet, which made for much better copy in dime novels.

Dr. Ephraim McDowell performed the first successful surgical removal of an ovarian tumor in Danville in 1809. And he did it without anesthesia, which didn't bother him but probably wasn't too much fun for his patient. You can see just how primitive this early surgery was—they didn't call physicians "sawbones" for nothing back then—with a visit to Dr. McDowell's office, which has been restored to its early nineteenth-century charm. Well, maybe not charm.

The McDowell House is at 125 South Second Street. Call (859) 236-2804 for information or visit www.mcdowellhouse.com.

The Most Famous Kentuckian (Non-Athlete's Division)
Frankfort

Without Daniel Boone, where would Kentuckians be? Probably in West Virginia. Born in Berks County, Pennsylvania, on November 2, 1734, to Squire Boone and the former Sarah Morgan, both Quakers, Daniel got a taste of life on the frontier at an early age. That's because his family was kicked out of genteel Berks County when Daniel was fifteen. It seems his father allowed son Israel to marry a non-Quaker. So the family hit the trail and relocated to Yadkin Valley, North Carolina.

In 1756 Boone married Rebecca Bryan, but he wasn't home much, which makes you wonder how they managed to have ten kids together. He was always off fighting Indians and conquering land as a frontiersman in what is now Kentucky.

Scholars believe that Boone first saw Kentucky from Pilot Knob in Powell County in 1769. In 1773 Boone failed at his first attempt to settle Kentucky. By 1775, however, he had finally succeeded and had established Boonesborough, a fort about 20 miles southwest of Lexington. But although Boone had finally found success, it was short-lived. Not known for his financial skills, Boone was swindled out of most of his money and the land he had fought for. Embittered, broke, and discouraged, Boone left Kentucky in 1820 to live with his son in Defiance, Missouri, stating that he was leaving because Kentucky "was too crowded."

Things didn't get easier for Boone after he moved. After his death a fight ensued between his family in Missouri and officials in Kentucky for his remains. Kentucky felt that Boone's final resting place should be in Frankfort, where citizens could pay homage to one of their founding fathers. Boone's family, on the other hand, felt his remains should stay in Missouri because Boone hated Kentucky. Ignoring the family, Kentucky officials traveled to Missouri, dug up the remains, and brought them back to Kentucky.

Or did they?

★ ★

At the time of Boone's death, he had wished to be buried next to his wife in Missouri. The only problem was that the burial plots next to her were already occupied. So his family buried him at the foot of his wife's grave. Knowing that Kentucky officials were coming to take Boone's remains, they didn't resist. They didn't tell them that they had the wrong body either. Kentucky officials proudly brought back the remains of the body next to Rebecca Boone.

In 1983 forensic anthropologist conducted a study on the remains

Quintessential Kentuckians

George Graham Vest—A Dog's Best Friend

Dog has always been man's best friend. It just took a Kentuckian to coin the famous phrase.

Frankfort native George Graham Vest was practicing law in Missouri in 1870 when he took on the case of Charles Burden, whose beloved hunting dog, Old Drum, had been shot by a sheep farmer named Leonidas Hornsby. Burden sued Hornsby in civil court for damages, and Vest gave his famous closing summation, "Tribute To the Dog":

The best friend a man has in this world may turn against him and become his enemy. His son or daughter that he has reared with loving care may prove ungrateful. Those who are nearest and dearest to us, those whom we trust with our happiness and our good name, may become traitors to their faith. The money that a man has, he may lose. It flies away from him, perhaps when he needs it most. . . . The one absolutely unselfish friend that a man

★ ★

in Frankfort to determine once and for all who had Daniel Boone's body. When the results came back from a plaster cast of the skull, it was determined that the remains in Frankfort belonged to a large black male. Frankfort officials deny the results and insist that they have the true remains of Daniel Boone. If nothing else, they have the largest tombstone.

Boone's bones may or may not be in his grave in Frankfort Cemetery, located at East Main Street.

can have in this selfish world, the one that never deserts him and the one that never proves ungrateful or treacherous is his dog. . . . Gentlemen of the jury, a man's dog stands by him in prosperity and in poverty, in health and in sickness. He will sleep on the cold ground, where the wintry winds blow and the snow drives fiercely, if only he may be near his master's side. If fortune drives the master forth an outcast in the world, friendless and homeless, the faithful dog asks no higher privilege than that of accompanying him to guard against danger, to fight against his enemies, and when the last scene of all comes and death takes the master in its embrace and his body is laid away in the cold ground, no matter if all other friends pursue their way, there by his graveside will the noble dog be found, his head between his paws, his eyes sad but open in alert watchfulness, faithful and true even to death.

Vest won $50 for his client. When copies of his speech began circulating, he won acclaim from dog lovers everywhere and in 1879 was elected to the United States Senate from Missouri. He served four terms.

★ ☆ ★ ☆ ★ ☆ ★ ☆ ★ ☆ ★ ☆ ★ ☆ ★ ☆ ★ ☆ ★ ☆ ★ ☆ ★ ☆ ★ ☆ ★ ☆ ★ ☆ ★ ☆ ★ ☆ ★

Whoa, Herry!
Harrodsburg

They say if you get up early enough and sit on the banks of Lake Herrington long enough, eventually you will see Herry. That's Herry the Lake Monster, Kentucky's answer to Nessie, Scotland's Loch Ness Monster. Herry was first spotted in 1972 by University of Kentucky classics professor Lawrence Thompson. Since then she's reared her ugly head—they say she looks like a catfish with PMS—at fishermen and picnickers. The consensus is that Herry is fifteen feet long with a pig snout and a curly tail and God knows what in between. She's seldom spotted after morning, the theory being that she's spooked by the powerboats that take over the lake when power-boaters finally wrest themselves from bed.

What is she, really? Some say she's a giant catfish; others believe she's nothing more than a bobbing bit of driftwood. And a few hold that she's a monster!

The Lake Herrington Monster has been spotted at Rocky Fork near Dix Dam and in the area between Lake Chenault and Wells Landing. Head to Burgin, just east of Harrodsburg. At the junction of Highways 33 and 152, take 33 north. A half-mile from the junction, when the road veers left, take Curdsville Road straight ahead for 2.5 miles. Turn right at the DIX DOCK sign. This is as close as you can get to Rocky Fork via land. It's off to the left out of sight. Meander over, sit down, and wait.

Buryin' the Hatchet
Lancaster

It must be something in the water. Kentucky, home of bourbon whiskey and burley tobacco, is also home to the most famous temperance crusader and the inventor of the most famous stop-smoking product. That would be Carrie A. Nation, "the lady with the hatchet," and Frank Etscorn, inventor of the nicotine patch.

Carry "Carrie" Amelia Moore Nation, born in Lancaster, Kentucky, was one of the first crusaders against alcohol. A brief marriage to an alcoholic in the late 1800s was enough to propel Nation to proclaim herself the perpetuator of prohibition. Hers was a quest of the heart, even if she did use force to enforce her beliefs against tobacco and alcohol, Kentucky's chief products. Nation once described herself as "a bulldog running along the feet of Jesus, barking at what he doesn't like."

Nation first "barked" at a bar in Kiowa, Kansas. With her faithful followers, mostly women who had been betrothed to drunks, Nation would barge into local watering holes, encouraging the women to destroy anything that stood in their way. As you can imagine, she wasn't too popular. Most bars would close when they got word that Nation was on her way. They didn't fear her message of prohibition as much as they feared her hatchet. Between 1900 and 1910 Nation was arrested more than thirty times. But her crusade eventually resulted in the passage of the Eighteenth Amendment and more than a decade of Prohibition (which eventually led to the Twenty-first Amendment: the repeal of Prohibition).

Hemp House
Lexington

This nineteenth-century plantation belonged to Lexington resident Henry Clay. Clay purchased the land in the early 1800s. The name Ashland refers to the Ash Forest that lay in the background of the house. The brick mansion housed Clay, his family, and slaves. One of those slaves was Charlotte Dupuy who met and married Aaron Dupuy, a slave held by Clay. The Dupuy family, which included two children, accompanied Clay, who was the secretary of state at the time, to Washington, D.C., where they experienced relative freedom. However, as Clay was beginning to leave Washington, D.C., Charlotte sued Clay for the emancipation of her and her children based on a previous agreement she made with her former owner. The court ultimately rejected her claim. This was seventeen years prior to the Dred Scott ruling. However, a little over ten years later Clay granted Charlotte and her children freedom. Today, the Clay home is a National Historic

★ ★

Landmark and a museum open to the public, though the hemp fields that once grew are no longer being cultivated.

The Henry Clay Estate is located at 120 Sycamore Road in Lexington. For more information check out the website at www.henryclay.org/ashland-estate.

It'll Always Be Burma to Me
Lexington

Until Thursday, May 18, 1995, *J. Peterman* was just another quirky catalog, a second-string player in a market dominated by Banana Republic, L. L. Bean, and J. Crew. But on that fateful night, Jerry Seinfeld's gal pal Elaine Benes landed a job writing catalog copy for an eccentric entrepreneur named J. Peterman (played by actor John O'Hurley), and soon everyone in America knew about the Peterman catalog.

The real J. Peterman isn't a Manhattan company but a small Lexington firm, and the real Mr. Peterman isn't a bombastic boss but a sensible businessman who, starting in 1987, built a catalog company based on his discoveries. *Seinfeld* creators Larry David and Jerry Seinfeld were fans of the catalog and created a character based on the voice in the catalog. And although no one bothered to inform the real John Peterman that his company was about to be satirized on the nation's number one television program in 1995, as the character caught on the *Seinfeld* folks made contact and eventually began sending advance scripts to the Kentucky businessman for his approval, which he gave.

Success spoiled J. Peterman. A too-rapid expansion into bricks-and-mortar retailing eventually sent the company into bankruptcy. John Peterman later bought back his name and company, and today the company is back in its old business—cranking out periodic catalogs (which the firm calls "Owner's Manuals") touting Gatsby shirts and Sussex armchairs, each hand-picked and guaranteed by one J. Peterman.

The offices of the J. Peterman Company are located at 1001 Primrose Court in Lexington. But J. Peterman learned the hard way about storefronts, so there isn't a company store—just the catalog, which is available at www.jpeterman.com. Phone (888) 647-2555.

Please, Mr. Postman

Next time you buy something via the United States Postal Service, thank Montgomery Blair. Blair, who was postmaster general under fellow Kentuckian Abraham Lincoln, was born in 1813 in Lexington. He left The Bluegrass for four years to study at West Point but returned in 1835 to get his law degree from Lexington's Transylvania College. He moved to Missouri to practice. It was there that he worked his most famous case: representing slave Dred Scott, whose petition for freedom was denied by the Supreme Court in 1857, paving the way for the Civil War. Even though Blair lost his case, his strong antislavery sympathies brought him to the attention of another Kentucky expatriate, Abraham Lincoln. In gratitude for fighting slavery—and for giving him his convention delegates—Lincoln named him postmaster general, a big-deal position at that time.

Blair was a clever fellow. In addition to inventing the money order, he established the first military post offices, improved international mail delivery, and abolished franking privileges for local postmasters (franking—free postage—was like a license to print stamps for the local postmasters). He was also the only cabinet officer to urge Lincoln to reinforce Fort Sumter in South Carolina, where the first shot of the Civil War was fired. He was a Lincoln loyalist who paid for his loyalty in the end. In 1864 radical Republican John Fremont was gearing up to challenge Lincoln in the presidential race. Fremont agreed to withdraw from the race if Lincoln would sack Blair. Lincoln would—and did.

Blair remained loyal to Lincoln's successor, Andrew Johnson, but when that got him nowhere, he switched to the Democratic Party. His name lives on today, with his former Washington residence, the Blair House, now owned by the government and used to house high-ranking foreign dignitaries when they visit this country.

★ ★

Inn of a Champion
Lexington

When he died in 1941, his death was reported in newspapers all over the world. He was identified as the World's Oldest and One of the World's Most Successful.

"He" was Merrick, a thirty-eight-year-old racehorse who had won sixty-one races in his ten-year career on the tracks of America.

In fact Merrick held the title of World's Oldest Horse in the *Guinness Book of World Records* for more than thirty years until he was displaced by the Australian thoroughbred Tango Duke, who lived to age forty-one.

But Merrick was more than just a reliable old racehorse—he ran in 205 races and finished in the money in 157 of them—he was a pal to

R.I.P. Noble Steed.

his owner J. Cal Milam. "No matter how long you have them, you're never ready to let them go," Milam grieved in the *Montreal Gazette* when Merrick passed away.

Milam had no children. He was so broken up over the death of his longtime pal—he had owned Merrick for thirty-five years, which is an eternity in the horse racing world—that he buried the gelding (meaning Merrick had no children either) in the front yard of his Lexington horse farm and renamed the estate Merrick Place.

Little did he know that years later his heirs would sell the farm to developers who would turn the house into a restaurant and surround it with apartment buildings, lots of apartment buildings.

So that's how it is that the Merrick Inn has a horse buried outside its front door.

It has nothing to do with the food, which is excellent, and has been for thirty years. The food is why it's a Lexington icon.

Get the Hot Brown, a delicious variation on the dish created at Louisville's Brown Hotel.

The Merrick Inn is located at 1074 Merrick Drive in Lexington. For more information check out the website at www.themerrickinn.com.

Just Like in the Movies
Lexington

Calumet Farm is what a horse farm should look like: white fences, rolling hills, grazing horses. In fact the farm has been the setting for a number of movies, including *Seabiscuit* and *Dreamer: Inspired by a True Story.*

The gorgeous 762-acre horse breeding and training farm, adjacent to Keeneland Race Course, has nineteen barns and its own dirt and turf practice tracks. Calumet has been home to such famed horses as Whirlaway, Citation, and Alydar.

The farm was established in the 1920s by William Monroe Wright, who named it after the manufacturing company he had founded, Calumet Baking Powder.

Originally a farm for trotters, the most popular type of racing horse at the time, the farm was converted to Thoroughbred breeding in the 1930s, after the original Mr. Wright died and his son, Warren, took over the farm.

Wright the younger hired Ben Jones as his trainer and the partnership produced an astounding eight Kentucky Derby winners between 1941 and 1968, more than any other operation in racing history.

Calumet fell on hard times in the late 1980s and declared bankruptcy in 1991. But even business downturns didn't affect the beauty of the place. It's still the horse farm of horse farms.

Today Calumet remains a private farm, but you can arrange group tours or private tours through a number of Lexington-area companies. While a private excursion is more expensive—$75 a person and up versus around $25 per person for a group tour—it's worth it if you can swing it.

You can find a list of tour companies at www.visitlex.com/quick/tours.html, including Blue Grass Tours (859-252-5744) and Kentucky Horse Tours (859-312-1124). For more information visit www.calumet farm.com.

Do I Hear $14 Million?
Lexington

It's the "prettiest little racetrack in America," according to Peter Fornatale, who should know. As the author of the horse-wagering book *Six Secrets of Successful Bettors: Winning Insights into Playing the Horses,* he's visited them all.

Keeneland is so pretty it doesn't even look like a racetrack. More like a hunting lodge with a track next to it. Its motto: "Racing as it was meant to be."

Keeneland Race Course has another side, the side you probably read more about in the papers, since Thoroughbreds only run on the track two months a year, April and October. It's the famous Keeneland horse sales, which have been held since World War II, when wartime

The race is on.

restrictions on rail transportation prevented Kentucky horse breeders from shipping their young colts to the Saratoga Horse Sales in New York. The first Keeneland yearling sale was August 9, 1943, and they've conducted a summer yearling sale every year since.

Today there are five sales a year—in January, April, July, September, and November—each for a different type of horse. The September sale, for instance, is for yearlings only. The November sale is for breeding stock. In 1985 a yearling named Seattle Dancer sold at Keeneland for $13 million. That's still the record and a lot of money for horseflesh.

★ ★

Keeneland's sales are open to the public. You won't get an up-close seat; those are reserved for buyers and their agents. But there is a spectator gallery in the back of the pavilion, just behind the reserved seating.

You can even bid, providing you have a credit application on file.

Keeneland is located at 4201 Versailles Road, which is also US Highway 60 (the Winchester Road exit off Interstate 75). It winds around and goes through downtown, but it's the easiest route if you don't know Lexington. For more information call (859) 254-3412 or (800) 456-3412 or visit www.keeneland.com.

The Daily (Mix and) Grind—Tools of the Trade
Lexington

There's a coffee shop in the shape of a giant coffee cup in Massachusetts and a hot dog stand in the shape of a giant wiener in Colorado. But as best I can determine, Bondurant Pharmacy in Lexington is the only drugstore in the world shaped like a giant mortar and pestle. And I think I would know—I wrote a book about drugstores (*Did Trojans Use Trojans?*).

And it is a *giant* mortar and pestle: thirty feet tall and thirty-two feet in diameter. The pestle juts skyward another ten feet.

The pharmacy is built in a style of architecture called "mimetic," something we don't have much of in Kentucky. "Mimetic" means the structure mimics a real object. In this case it mimics a now almost-obsolete tool of the druggist trade, the mortar and pestle, which pharmacists once used to grind pills and potions. Today almost all medicine arrives in the drugstore in a prepared form. The pharmacist only needs to count out the pills.

Bondurant Pharmacy was built in 1975 according to a design that was patented by founder and pharmacist Joseph Bondurant. Bondurant took what had been the drugstore symbol for years and turned it into a blueprint. In keeping with the theme, the store's directional signs are also in the shape of a mortar and pestle. Inside it's just like any other pharmacy. But outside it's a sight.

Mortar and pestle from bricks and mortar.

Bondurant Pharmacy is no longer open but the unique building still stands at 1465 Village Drive, just off US Highway 60. You can get there by taking US Highway 60 west (Winchester Road) off Interstate 75 and sticking with it through downtown. The phone number is (859) 254-8852.

★ ★

Kentucky's Wright Stuff

Lexington

Let's be honest. When you think of aviation history, you think of Kitty Hawk, North Carolina, where the Wright Brothers flew the first powered aircraft, or Dayton, Ohio, where the two Wrights lived and experimented. You don't exactly think of Kentucky. But Kentucky has a place, a small place perhaps, in aviation history.

A Kentuckian invented the parachute with a ripcord and an airplane ejection seat. A Kentuckian was the first African-American woman to get a private pilot's license. And a Kentuckian invented and flew the first plane with retractable landing gear.

It was Solomon Van Meter of Lexington—obviously a cautious type—who invented the ripcord and the ejection seat. Willa Brown Chappell of Glasgow, Kentucky, was the first black female private pilot. And Matthew Sellers was living near Grayson, east of Lexington, when he perfected his retractable landing gear, a mere five years after the Wrights' first flight.

You can learn more about these three aviation history makers at the Aviation Museum of Kentucky, which is located at Bluegrass Airport at the intersection of Man O' War Boulevard and US Highway 60. Phone (859) 231-1219 or visit the website at www.aviationky.org.

I See Red! I Taste Purple!

Lexington

Between 1953 and 1962 government doctors tested the psychedelic drug LSD on three hundred human patients, prisoners who were being treated for drug addiction at the US Public Service Hospital in Bracktown. The experiments were funded, just barely, by the CIA. Because there was no money to pay the prisoners for their participation, they were given a choice of time off their sentences or the drug of their choice. Most chose drugs. One prisoner told a senate subcommittee

Just say no to time off!

that he received morphine for his participation. Pennsylvania Senator Richard Schweicker replied, "I understand now why the percentage of cure at Lexington may not have been too high."

From Lexington take US Highway 421, Leestown Pike, north. The old hospital is on the right, just past Masterson Station Park. It is now the Federal Correction Institute. You can see all you need to from the road.

★ ★

Frankly, Scarlett, I'll Stay at Belle's

Lexington

She's just about the most famous hooker in history—having taken Rhett Butler in when Scarlett tossed him out. The character of Belle Watling was based on Belle Brezing, a Kentucky madam famed for her luxurious brothel, her influential clientele, and the business acumen that gave her a reputation for running "the most orderly of disorderly houses."

Brezing was too young to host soldiers during the Civil War—she was born in Lexington in 1860—but she lived the life for thirty-eight years, from 1879, when she moved into the Jenny Hill brothel, which was housed in the building where Mary Todd Lincoln grew up, till the army closed her down in 1917.

She opened her own brothel in a rented row house on North Upper Street across from Transylvania University on July 1, 1881. Over the next four decades she variously operated houses at 194 North Upper Street and at 59 Megowan Street. And when she was convicted of running a house of ill repute in 1882, Governor Luke P. Blackburn pardoned her. Hmmmm, interesting that.

Her claim to fame, or infamy, during her career was that she was indicted more times than any other citizen in Lexington. Belle died in 1940. On her cemetery monument is this simple epitaph: BLESSED ARE THE PURE IN HEART.

Belle Brezing is buried in Calvary Cemetery, Section O, Lot 6. None of her famed "houses" remain. The most notorious was at the corner of Wilson and Megowan. Calvary Cemetery is at 874 West Main Street. From Interstate 75 take exit 116 for Paris Road. It becomes North Broadway, which runs into Main. Turn right on Main.

Willst Thou Liveth behind a Moat?
Lexington

First-time cruisers on Lexington's Versailles Road often come to a screeching halt when they round the bend near the airport. They think they've hit a time warp because there on the north side of the highway is a giant castle, complete with stone walls, turrets, drawbridge, and moat. All that's missing is a knight in shining armor—or a band of disgruntled villagers with torches beseeching m'lord for lower taxes.

There are rumors that the castle was to be a modern-day fairy-tale home for a twentieth-century Lancelot and Guinevere. Or that its owners moved out because it was haunted.

Here's the real story: Rex and Caroline Martin got the idea for a castle during a European vacation in 1968. They purchased fifty-three

Be it ever so humble.

acres on US Highway 60 outside Lexington and broke ground in 1969. Their finished estate was to have seven bedrooms, fifteen baths, four corner towers, a dozen turrets, twelve-foot-high walls, a drawbridge, an Italian fountain in the courtyard, and tennis courts in back. But before the castle could be completed, the couple divorced, leaving the place unfinished and empty—and now unsold.

In 1988 the publicity-shy Rex Martin put the castle on the market with a FOR SALE sign that also said APPOINTMENT ONLY and gave a phone number that no one ever answered. Martin died in 2003 without ever selling the castle. His estate sold it to a Florida couple who were in the process of converting it to a bed and breakfast when a lightning strike set the house on fire. It has since been rebuilt to its original glory and turned into a tourist inn.

The site is on Versailles Road, west of Keeneland Race Course, near the Woodford County line. For more information check out the website at www.thecastlepost.com/default.asp.

Which One of You Is Sybil?
Lexington

If you've seen the 1976 TV movie, the one Sally Fields won an Emmy for, you know all about multiple-personality sufferer Sybil Dorsett. The movie, *Sybil,* was based on the 1973 best-selling book of the same name, which, in turn, was based on the real life story of Shirley Ardell Mason, who lived quietly in Lexington the last two decades of her life. A few of her Lexington neighbors had their suspicions. After all, Dr. Cornelia Wilbur, a University of Kentucky professor identified in the book as Sybil's psychiatrist, was an almost daily visitor to the Mason home. But most knew Mason as a quiet woman who spent her days dabbing at her watercolor paintings and managing an art and antiques business out of her home.

But *Sybil* was more than just a movie. Before the film was shown, "multiple-personality disorder" was considered a rare mental disorder; the American Psychiatric Association didn't even list it as a distinct disease. After the movie there was a boom in reported multiple-personality cases. Thanks, Sybil—and Sybil and Sybil and Sybil and . . .

Mason lived at 345 Henry Clay Boulevard. It is now a private residence.

"Know What I Mean, Vern?"

If you have children, or if you are a child, then you know Ernest. That's Ernest P. Worrell, Esquire Deluxe, for those who don't. Ernest is the annoying but good-hearted soul who saves the world and Santa and the kids in the neighborhood in a string of Ernest comedies that came from Disney Studios in the 1980s and '90s.

The Ernest character was created out of whole cloth by a Lexington native, the late Jim Varney. Varney sort of practiced for the Ernest part as a semiregular on the late 1970s TV series, *America 2-Night,* a spinoff of *Mary Hartman, Mary Hartman.* He played the recurring character of mobile home daredevil Virgil Sims, an early incarnation of Ernest P. if there ever was one. The long-faced Virgil would appear on the talk show spoof periodically to boast of his recent exploits: He would jump his mobile home over an increasing number of cars.

When he was hired for a commercial touting Beech Bend Park in western Kentucky, he created Ernest P. The park went under, but Varney's career went straight up. There were nine Ernest comedies in all, each one more outrageous than the next.

In a 1984 interview Varney described how he found the Ernest P. in himself. He confided that he grew up around quite a few Ernest P. Worrells in Kentucky. "They kind of flourish in this part of the country." Varney died on February 10, 2000.

★ ★

Kentucky's "First" Lady

Lexington

Sophonisba Preston Breckinridge—and yes, that is a mouthful—has a lot of firsts after her name. She was both the first woman to receive a PhD in political science and the first woman admitted to the Kentucky Bar. But her proudest first was the one that was the longest coming: She was arguably the first social worker and single-handedly invented the profession of social work.

Born into a socially prominent Lexington family, Breckinridge graduated from Wellesley College and settled in Washington, D.C., where she taught high school math. But she was restless, and after taking a year off to make the Grand Tour of Europe, she returned to Lexington to study law in her father's law office. She passed the bar, but a year in a law office convinced her that being a lawyer wasn't her calling either. Then an old college chum invited her to live in Chicago. She jumped at the offer, eventually landing a job in the dean's office at the University of Chicago. With Dean Marion Talbot's help, in 1901 Breckinridge became the first woman to receive a doctoral degree in political science. Restless still, she never pursued a career in politics.

Then in 1906 she began researching employment patterns of women, comparing census data and court records in her quest to determine why some households produced "troubled" kids. The research formed the basis of her book *Back of the Yards,* a study that explored the relationship between public housing and crime and led her to her final destination—a career working with the socially disadvantaged, a field she named "social work."

One of her final firsts: creating the School of Civics and Philanthropy at University of Chicago, a department school that was later renamed the Department of Social Service Administration. It should be renamed the Sophonisba Preston Breckinridge Department of Social Service Administration. But that may be too much of a mouthful.

Big Red

Lexington

He was the Muhammad Ali of horseracing. The Greatest. In fact he may even have been *more* famous than Muhammad Ali. Let's face it: There wasn't all that much to capture the national attention in the 1920s anyway.

His name was Man O' War. He was so famous they even named a road in Lexington after him. What did he do that brought him such fame?

For starters "Big Red," as he was known, won twenty times in twenty-one starts, despite racing only two seasons. He set five world records, even though his handicap was frequently as high as 138 pounds, unheard of today. For comparison's sake, horses in the Kentucky Derby now carry 126 pounds. He won one race, the Lawrence Realization, by one hundred lengths. His only loss was in the Sanford Stakes at Saratoga; he was carrying 130 pounds, fifteen pounds more than the next closest horse. The big chestnut was backing up when the starter's gun went off, leaving him in the dust. He almost made it up, losing by a mere half-length to a horse named Upset. He would beat Upset six times in his career.

When Man O' War died in 1947, he was embalmed and laid out in a custom casket. His funeral was broadcast nationwide on the Mutual Radio Network. Two thousand people attended, and nine different people delivered eulogies. He achieved all this fame despite never winning the Kentucky Derby. (He never ran in the most famous of horse races because his trainer thought it too early in the year to run a mile and a quarter.)

He was a champion off the track as well, siring 379 offspring, including Triple Crown winner War Admiral and the beloved Seabiscuit.

A bronze statue of Man O' War stands over his grave in the Kentucky Horse Park. The park is located off Interstate 75 at exit 120, four miles north of Lexington. Call (800) 678-8813 for information or visit www.kyhorsepark.com.

★ ★

Mother of All Pancakes
Mount Sterling

Most states would be proud to have one famous packaged cooking mix call the place home. Kentucky can be doubly proud: We are home to two famous mix masters. Duncan Hines, the guy who lent his name to cake mix, is from Bowling Green (see The Pennyrile chapter). And Nancy Green, better known as Aunt Jemima of pancake mix fame, is from Mount Sterling. Of course neither actually invented the mix that bears his or her name. But that's another story.

Green, a former slave whose face was on pancake mix boxes all over America and became advertising's first living trademark, was born in 1834 in Montgomery County. Green was a renowned cook, but she didn't invent her namesake pancake mix. That credit goes to a couple of white men, Chris L. Rutt and Charles G. Underwood, who bought the Pearl Milling Company of St. Joseph, Missouri, in the 1880s. They weren't planning on being millers. They had bigger ideas; they wanted a product. Packaged food was becoming all the rage—witness the popularity of pre-packaged cereal by the Kellogg Brothers of Battle Creek, Michigan—and they hit upon the idea of a ready-mixed, self-rising pancake flour. The name for their product came from a chance evening Rutt spent at a minstrel show where he saw a performer in apron and bandana sing a catchy tune named "Aunt Jemima." As he exited the theater, everyone was humming the song, and he knew he had a name for his pancake mix. While Rutt and Underwood were long on imagination, they were short on cash and went broke—but not before selling their pancake product to the R. T. Davis Milling Company in 1890.

Davis decided he needed a spokeswoman. He found Nancy Green in Chicago, where she was the housekeeper for a judge and where the World's Columbian Exposition was being held in 1893. There Davis put her in front of the world's largest flour barrel and instructed her to play the part of Aunt Jemima. She did, charming the crowd so much that fair officials had to hire extra policemen to keep the throngs moving in front of the booth. Davis put Green on the road, and she spent the next thirty years, until her death in 1923 in Chicago at age eighty-nine, promoting pancakes. Her image lives on today on the pancake mix box that bears her "adopted" name, Aunt Jemima. Yes, it's been updated so that Aunt Jemima has lost the bandana, but look closely and you can still see Nancy Green's smile.

A Courtin' We Will Go

Mount Sterling

What brings more than 100,000 people to eastern Kentucky for three days in October? Guns. But it's not hunting season. It's trading season, and the occasion is the largest swap meet in the state: Court Day.

Every year, the third Monday in October is declared Court Day in Mount Sterling. But because this is Kentucky, Court Day is more than just one day: It's also the Saturday and Sunday preceding the third Monday of October.

Court Day began at the turn of the nineteenth century when the General Assembly passed a law that said each county should meet at least once a month to handle all court and business affairs. Due to its location between neighboring counties, Mount Sterling became a trading-post mecca. People from all over gathered for three days to trade mules, turkeys, geese, trapped wild animals, sorghum molasses, vegetables, ponies, horses, and, of course, guns. Hey, our founding father is Daniel Boone after all.

Gone are the mules, horses, and other livestock, but you can still find plenty of fresh produce, crafts, and country goods. The biggest draw to the festival now is guns. If you ask the right people, though, you could probably still find a mule. There's a reason why Mount Sterling's motto is "Where the bluegrass meets the mountains."

For more information on Court Day, call (859) 498-8732 or visit www.mountsterling-ky.com/courtday.

Petticoats and Slide Rules

All her life Margaret Ingels wanted to be an architect. But when she arrived at the University of Kentucky from her Paris (Kentucky, not France) home in 1910, she discovered the school had no architectural program. Dean F. Paul Anderson convinced her to try mechanical engineering as "the next best thing." It was a perfect fit. She graduated in 1916 and four years later became the first female to receive the professional degree of Mechanical Engineer.

She worked for the Chicago Telephone Company for a time before joining Carrier Engineering in Pittsburgh, where she began her lifelong love affair with "conditioned air." In 1921 she joined the American Society of Heating and Ventilating Engineers research lab to work on the development of air-conditioning. She became a spokesperson for the mechanical engineering profession, speaking to more than 12,000 people over two decades, delivering a speech she called "Petticoats and Slide Rules."

"The woman who joins the procession of engineers today, tomorrow, and tomorrow's tomorrow benefits by a rich heritage bequeathed to her by those who came before. She assumes automatically the responsibility to further prove that petticoats and slide rules are compatible, and she must not carry the responsibility lightly. Her task is to widen the trails blazed for her—and more. She must build them into great highways for women engineers of the future to travel, free of prejudices and discrimination."

Ingels was inducted into the College of Engineering Hall of Distinction in 1993. As they say in the air-conditioning field: cool!

See McGuffey Write

Paris

In 1823 Pennsylvania native William Holmes McGuffey was just a pup, a mere twenty-three, when he hired on at the Paris subscription school, located in a converted smokehouse. McGuffey wrote to his brother that he was assembling his reading book because so few of the students in his classroom could read. He remained for four years, putting his off-hours to good use as he assembled a collage of poems, essays, short stories, and speeches.

First published in 1836, the Readers—the first was known as the *Peerless Pioneer* Reader—were wildly popular, eventually selling more than 120 million copies. While the books had a reputation for having a stern tone, McGuffey drew on all manner of literature, from Dickens to Longfellow, to make his books fun to read. The six McGuffey Readers became one of the most widely read series of books in nineteenth-century America and among the most influential.

The school/smokehouse is gone. It was located on High Street on the south side of Public Square in downtown Paris. There's a historical marker to guide you to the site.

Birth of the Baptists

Cane Ridge, Near Paris

The Baptists were born in Kentucky—along with the Methodists, the Disciples of Christ, the Pentecostals, the Holy Rollers, and almost every religion that depends on fervor from its congregation.

Okay, they weren't literally born here; they were all founded elsewhere. But an event on the Kentucky prairie two centuries ago rejuvenated what had been fringe religions. It happened in 1801 in the Cane Ridge Meeting House, a meeting hall that is said to be the largest one-room log building in North America, measuring forty by sixty feet.

Paul Conkin, former head of the history department at Vanderbilt University and author of *Cane Ridge: America's Pentecost* (and my first cousin, I should note, in the interest of full disclosure), calls the religious gathering at Cane Ridge "the most important religious gathering in all of American history, both for what it symbolized and the effects that flowed from it."

More than 20,000 people gathered around that log building in August 1801 to hear preachers and orators and fire-and-brimstone sermons. Many lay down on the ground and shook from their newborn religious fervor. Hands were laid on, offerings were collected, souls were given over. It was one phenomenal gathering: For six days that tiny spot was Kentucky's largest city. One eyewitness, James Finley, wrote in his biography that "the noise was like the roar of Niagara. At one time I saw at least 500 swept down in a moment as if a battery of a thousand guns had been opened upon them, and then immediately followed shrieks and shouts that rent the very heavens."

But it was more than a religious revival; it was also a social gathering, the first in the new state's history (Kentucky was a mere nine years old). Some souls weren't just saved, they were married. Nine months after Cane Ridge, Kentucky experienced its first baby boom.

The Cane Ridge Meeting House is eight miles east of Paris, Kentucky. Take US Highway 460 East to Highway 537. For information call (859) 987-5350 or visit www.caneridge.org.

Stop! Birthplace of the Man Who Invented the Traffic Light
Paris

If Garrett Morgan had never lived, what a mess traffic would be in! It was Morgan who invented the traffic light, a mechanism that made it safe for motorists to approach an intersection.

Morgan, who was born on a farm in Paris to two former slaves, was always a tinkerer. So when he moved to Cleveland, Ohio, in 1895 he had no trouble landing a job as a repairman at a sewing machine manufacturer. Because he was so good he soon had his own repair company. While driving to work one day, he witnessed as a car and a horse-drawn carriage both charged into an intersection. The resulting collision gave him an idea. He sketched the design for a T-shaped pole with three signs on it: stop, go, and a third sign that stopped traffic in all directions so pedestrians could cross. He patented his invention in 1923, and soon Morgan Traffic Signals were all over the country. GE, Thomas Edison's company, was so impressed that it bought Morgan's patent for $40,000. Morgan sold out just in time, because the tri-colored traffic light soon supplanted his invention.

Morgan never stopped experimenting and later invented a zigzag stitching attachment for sewing machines and a gas mask. He attracted national attention when he donned the mask and rescued several men trapped by an explosion in an underground tunnel beneath Lake Erie. The Morgan gas mask was later adopted by the US Army during World War I and by fire departments all across the country.

Float Like a Pair of Butterflies: The Two Cassius Clays
Richmond

Although they were born more than a century apart, people continue to confuse Kentucky's two Cassius Clays. In fact, back in the nineties, Lexington's WKYT television station produced a documentary on White Hall, the historic home of famed nineteenth-century abolitionist Cassius Clay. When the program was listed in *TV Guide,* an editor spotted what he thought was an error and changed the show's synopsis to reflect that White Hall was the former home of Muhammad Ali.

That's the problem we have in Kentucky: two, two, two famous Cassius Marcellus Clays. The first Cassius Marcellus Clay, born 1810, was a man of many accomplishments: He was a newspaper publisher, a naturalist, a founder of the national Republican Party, and an orator—an occupation that no longer exists (modern equivalent of an orator: a motivational speaker minus the tapes, the books, and the infomercials). From 1861 to 1869 he was US minister to Russia. He is even credited with convincing President Abraham Lincoln to sign the Emancipation Proclamation. Like a true Kentuckian, at age eighty-four this first Cassius Clay married a fifteen-year-old girl.

The second Cassius Marcellus Clay, born in Louisville in 1942, was a boxer—but not just any boxer. He was the self-proclaimed Greatest, and he may just have been. For certain he was the most colorful boxer

★ ★

of all time. He was also a man of many accomplishments—Olympic champion, three-time heavyweight champion—and an orator in his own right. His boxing philosophy: "The fight is won or lost far away from witnesses—behind the lines, in the gym, and out there on the road, long before I dance under those lights."

From Future City to Rabbit Hash—Weird-Named Kentucky Towns

When out-of-staters ask where Paducah is, locals have a little joke. They say, "It's halfway between Monkeys Eyebrow and Possum Trot." And it is. Monkeys Eyebrow is a defunct community in Ballard County, west of Paducah, and Possum Trot is a dot on the map in Marshall County, to the east. Also nearby are Fancy Farm, in Graves County, and the town of Oscar in Ballard County.

In Kentucky we love giving our towns names that will cause a stranger to bolt upright in surprise . . . or delight. Take Rabbit Hash. It's nothing more than a general store in Boone County, on Highway 536 just southwest from Cincinnati. The name supposedly derives from the recipe that helped a group of folks survive a particularly harsh flood in 1816. (The store is at 10021 Lower River Road; 859-586-7744.)

Future City, near Kevil in Ballard County, supposedly got its name from the developer who was going to build a town, put up the sign—Future City—but never got around to building anything. Then

In 1964 Clay the boxer changed his name to Muhammad Ali to reflect his embrace of the Muslim faith. Though he retired from boxing in 1981, he remains one of the most famous people in the world.

White Hall is located at 500 White Hall Shrine Road in Richmond. Take exit 95 east from Interstate 75. Call (859) 623-9178 for information.

there's 88, Kentucky, in Barren County (on Highway 90, seven miles south of Glasgow), which supposedly got its name because one of the founders had 88 cents in his pocket when they were trying to pick a name. At least that's one story. Robert M. Rennick, who traced the names of hundreds of our towns for his 1984 book, *Kentucky Place Names*, offers a different one: The local postmaster had such poor handwriting that he picked the name because he was sure everyone could read his rendering of those two numerals.

Mud Lick doesn't sound too strange. A bit nasty, but not strange. Maybe that explains why there are nine towns with that name in Kentucky: in Anderson, Elliott, Greenup, Knox, Lewis, Robertson, Russell, Perry, and Pike Counties. What does sound disgusting is Paint Lick, a town on Highway 52 in Garrard County. Turns out it's not so bad: It was a salt lick marked for prime hunting by Indians, who painted nearby rocks to mark the spot.

There are two Lambs, one in Kenton County and another in Monroe County. There's no explanation for the town of Typo in Perry County. But you could make up a good story. Bush, Kentucky, in the mountains of Laurel County, was named for George Bush—just not the one you think. The original George Bush founded the town in 1840, when he opened a post office in the general store. The town's

(Continued on next page)

(Continued from previous page)

original name was Bush's Store. And when the first President Bush campaigned there in 1988, the headline read "Bush Returns to Bush."

Other curious town names in Kentucky:

- **Black Gnat** (Taylor County)
- **Black Snake** (Bell County)
- **Co-operative** (McCreary County)
- **Crummies** (Harlan County)
- **Hi Hat** (Floyd County)
- **Quality** (Butler County)
- **Subtle** (Metcalfe County)
- **Susie** (Wayne County)
- **Whoopee Hill** (Ohio County)
- **Wild Cat** (Clay County)

Most everyone's favorite Kentucky town name is Bugtussle, on Highway 87 south of Tompkinsville in Monroe County, near the Tennessee border. Fans of *The Beverly Hillbillies* may recall that the Clampetts were from Bugtussle, albeit Bugtussle, Tennessee.

The name, long a synonym for a backwater town, conjures up images of a couple of cockroaches going at it in a wrestling ring. Rennick found a source that claimed the name came from the time of traveling wheat thrashers, who stayed so long sleeping in beds of hay that the bedbugs got huge and began tussling in the bed.

So what about Monkeys Eyebrow and Possum Trot?

Monkeys Eyebrow, which is spelled without the apostrophe, is no more. It was founded at the beginning of the twentieth century by a couple of brothers, John and Dodge Ray, who opened a store on Sand Ridge, some fifteen miles west of Wickliffe. The community never had a post office, so it never really mattered where the name came from. But there are numerous tales, most of which have to do with a topographical feature that resembles a monkey's eyebrow. The least likely, but most interesting, was recorded by a WPA researcher, who heard that an ornery local claimed his neighbors in the area "belong to the monkey class."

To see where Monkeys Eyebrow used to be, take Highway 473 from Bandana through Ogden. Monkeys Eyebrow once was shortly before the junction with Highway 1105.

Possum Trot supposedly got its name when US Highway 62 was under construction in the early years of the twentieth century. After a morning of fruitless hunting, one local told his companion that if they didn't get a possum soon, the possums were going to trot across the road and escape.

Possum Trot is at the intersection of US Highway 62 and Highway 1610.

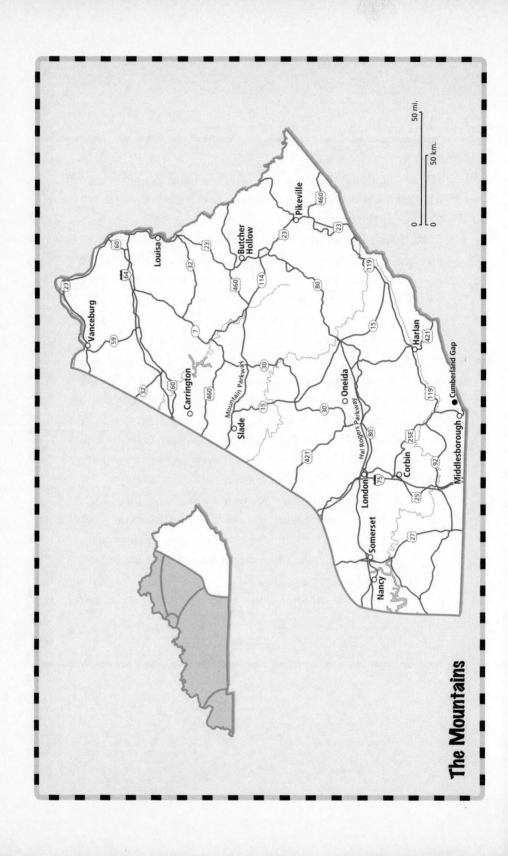

The Mountains

3

The Mountains

When people outside of Kentucky think of Kentuckians, most think of a tobacco-chewing, toothless illiterate with raggedy clothes, a flint-lock musket, and a whiskey still behind a tumbledown cabin—a hillbilly, in other words. That's the image they've seen on TV and in comic strips ("Snuffy Smith") over the years. Okay, there are people in the moun-tains who have poor dental hygiene, no reading skills, and a strong love of illegal drink. But that doesn't begin to touch the diversity of the population.

TV, and in particular satellite TV, has brought the outside world to the hollers and hilltops of the Appalachian Mountains (and if you hear someone pronounce it ap-uh-LAY-chuns instead of ap-uh-LATCH-uns, be assured they aren't from around here). Mountain folk aren't isolated anymore.

In the mountains we now have mansions and luxury cars and satel-lite dishes. In fact the owner of the largest private collection of Rolls Royce cars is or was a Kentucky mountaineer. (Maybe you saw the story on 60 Minutes. He was a coalmine owner back in the heyday of coal mining.) There aren't many illegal stills left. The major illicit export is no longer moonshine—it's marijuana.

The modern world has arrived in the mountains. In fact it got here several decades ago; it just took the media a while to figure that out. Now some of the most respected writers and artists and businesspeople in the world are from our mountains.

It's Raining . . . Meat?

It was a clear, cloudless March day in 1876. Homemaker Mrs. Allan Crouch was in the yard of her Bath County farm making soap when she felt something smack her on the head. She rubbed the smarting spot and found blood—but not her own. It was blood from the falling object. She was pummeled by falling meat, in what would later be called the Famous Meat Shower. It was thin-sliced, and when it was all over, what amounted to a horse wagon full of the stuff had fallen on her yard.

There were no tornadoes or storms of any kind in the area that could have carried the meat to her home in the shadow of Carrington Rock. It was a good quarter century before the Wright Brothers, so the stuff couldn't have been dumped by an aircraft. The Famous Meat Shower was investigated by a team of professors from Transylvania College in Lexington, but no explanation was ever found.

Carrington Rock is located three miles south of Olympia Springs on Highway 36.

Kyle Campbell, Pole Bending Champion
Corbin

Knox County is the home of Kyle Campbell, 1999 world amateur pole bending champion. At least that's what the sign out on the bypass proclaims. Lest you think it's a joke, let me take this opportunity to set you straight. Kyle Campbell is, or was, the 1999 World Amateur Pole Bending Champion. But pole bending is not what you think. It doesn't involve musclemen hanging around a motel ballroom, taking turns bending ever-stiffer metal poles. Pole bending is an equestrian event.

HOME OF KYLE CAMPBELL
1999 WORLD AMATEUR
POLE BENDING CHAMPION

How many people would you have to beat?

That's right: Horses are involved.

Its closest relative is barrel racing, which you've probably seen on Sunday-morning TV. But instead of racing horses around barrels, competitors race their mounts around poles, six of them in all, that are six feet high and positioned twenty-one feet apart.

It's a very difficult event. Your horse must change leads (lead foot) while making this serpentine run through pole after pole. Not just anyone can excel at pole bending. But Kyle Campbell can and did in 1999, when he won the World Amateur event.

Salute him as you drive past his roadside monument on US Highway 25 just east of Corbin.

★ ★

Family Feud

The longest feud in US history belongs to Kentucky. No, I'm not talking about the Hatfields and McCoys. They settled their dispute long ago, after a few decades of squabbling. I'm talking about Brownie, Kentucky's Everly Brothers, Don and Phil, early rock-and-roll stars who had huge hits with "Wake Up Little Susie," "Bye Bye Love," and "Cathy's Clown."

But growing up together and singing together and touring together and starting a record label together took its toll. In 1973 Phil smashed his guitar during a concert and walked off the stage, leaving Don to explain to the audience that the two were through. "The Everly Brothers died ten years ago," he announced to the stunned audience.

The brothers reunited in 1983 as a singing duo, but not as pals. They still perform on stage together, but lest you think they've left that feud behind, understand that they still ride to their performances in separate limos. If the Everly Brothers died in '63, as Don told that audience, then they are in their fifth decade of feuding.

Finger Lickin' Good
Corbin

Kentucky has many stories of men and their chickens. Most of those stories, however, are not fit to print. One man, though, stands apart from the others—a man with a vision, a man who achieved worldwide fame and success. That chicken-loving man was Colonel Harland Sanders.

Sanders, or "the Colonel" as he is better known, didn't begin his chicken career until he was forty. The Colonel owned a service station

What came first, the chicken or the egg? In Kentucky it's definitely the chicken.

in Corbin, where he got the bright idea that he could make a little extra money if he could somehow combine his service station with a restaurant.

With that mission in mind, the Colonel opened his restaurant within the service station, using his own dining room table. He could seat only six, but it was six more than he had before. As he served home-cooked meals, the Colonel's reputation grew. Soon he was able to open the Sanders Cafe in 1937, which seated 142 customers. The Colonel was moving up!

★ ★

All the while he was working the service station and cafe, the Colonel was also working to perfect his "secret" recipe of eleven herbs and spices. He also experimented with ways to cook the chicken faster, designing a pressure cooker.

Colonel Sanders by the Numbers

6: Seats in Harland Sanders's first restaurant—his own dining room table in the living quarters of his Corbin service station

11: Herbs and spices in the Colonel's secret recipe for fried chicken

40: The Colonel's age when he started developing his secret recipe

65: The Colonel's age when he began franchising his chicken recipe

600: Kentucky Fried Chicken franchises in 1964

2 million Dollars John Y. Brown and Jack Massey paid Sanders for his business in 1964

11,000: Kentucky Fried Chicken restaurants around the world in 2006

2 billion: Kentucky Fried Chicken dinners served annually

9: Pieces of KFC Chicken consumed annually by every man, woman, and child in the US

2: Rank of Colonel Sanders in 1976 among world's most recognizable faces

In 1960 the Colonel franchised the Kentucky Fried Chicken (KFC) restaurant chain. By 1964 there were more than six hundred restaurants. The Colonel's popularity and image grew fast. By 1976 the Colonel's mug was so popular that he was voted the second most recognizable celebrity in the world.

The Colonel died on December 16, 1980. The man most people identified with the state of Kentucky through his KFC restaurants was given a state funeral, complete with visitation in the state Capitol in Frankfort. He was buried in Louisville's Cave Hill Cemetery.

It should be noted that old-timers in Corbin will tell you that locally the Colonel wasn't famous for his fried chicken, but for his country ham.

A Kentucky Fried Chicken restaurant is located inside Sanders Cafe, on US Highway 25 West. The only admission is a healthy appetite. Call (606) 528-2163 for current restaurant hours. There's also a Colonel Sanders Museum at KFC headquarters in Louisville (1441 Gardiner Lane; 502-874-8300).

"The Gators Got Your Granny"—Poke Sallet Festival
Harlan

Thanks to Tony Joe White at least a few people have heard of poke sallet. They think it's a salad and it was invented by Annie—thus his 1969 hit record "Poke Salad Annie"—but at least they are in the ballpark.

Actually it's a weed, not "the" weed, but a weed nonetheless, and every spring the folks of Harlan celebrate it with the Poke Sallet Festival.

Poke sallet has been a food staple for mountain people since the Depression. Food was scarce, and money to buy it was even harder to come by. Then someone stumbled upon this weed that grew in abundance in abandoned coalmines. It looks like a green, and some say tastes similar to a green, so they ate it. Thus began the culinary history of the poke sallet. In tribute, every year the festival has a poke sallet cooking contest, where chefs compete for best recipe.

Most natives and regular poke sallet eaters agree that the best way to cook it is to fry it in bacon grease. Before you grab a fork and dig in,

★ ★

however, be forewarned: The root and berry of the poke sallet are poisonous. Most mountain people don't believe this, though, and state that if it hasn't killed them yet, there's no harm.

For more information call (606) 573-4717 or visit www.harlan festivals.com/poke_sallet.htm.

Coal Miner's Daughter

She really was a coal miner's daughter. She really was married at thirteen, a mother at fifteen, and a grandmother at twenty-nine. But she made something of her life despite these obstacles.

Loretta Lynn wouldn't take no for an answer, and through sheer force of will—and a lot of shoe leather—became the biggest star in country music during the 1960s and '70s. The Kentucky native (born in the tiny town of Butcher Hollow) had a string of hits, some seventy in all during that period, including such hard-edged country songs as "Don't Come Home a Drinkin' (With Lovin' on Your Mind)," "You Ain't Woman Enough (To Take My Man)," and "I'm a Honky Tonk Girl." The girl had an attitude long before it was fashionable.

Her husband, Mooney, once said that the two of them drove 80,000 miles to sell 50,000 copies of her first record in 1959, but it paid off. That song, "I'm a Honky Tonk Girl," made it to number 14 on the country charts and established Lynn as a star. She would go on to record twenty-six number one country hits.

Born in 1934, Lynn is now collecting Social Security checks along with her royalty checks—and still recording. In fact her 2004 release, *Van Lear Rose,* won the Grammy for Best Country Music Album.

★ ★

Kentucky's Mother Lode

Johnson County (or Is It Martin County?)

John Swift was a sailor and an adventurer who on his deathbed in Virginia in the late 1700s told a tale of incalculable wealth. Swift related how he and his friend, George Munday, were partners in a Kentucky silver mine, the Kentucky Mother Lode. Oh, and what a lode it was—the vein was three feet high. Swift and Munday had had a falling out; he killed Munday, then turned to smelting all the silver for himself. He worked for fifteen months, then crated the silver up and hid it in a cave in the Appalachian Mountains of eastern Kentucky.

Swift made his way back to his hometown of Alexandria, Virginia, seeking help in retrieving his fortune. But no one believed him. Just another crazy old man, they said, and Swift died blind and penniless.

But not everyone doubted his tale. Over the years hundreds of fortune hunters have made their way to the mountains, searching for this cave located in the shadow of a "peculiar looking rock"—a stone supposedly shaped like a turtle with markings resembling turkey tracks on top.

No one has ever found it.

That's one version of the story. Others have the mine or mines in Virginia or Tennessee or North Carolina. But all agree on one thing: There's a fabulous load of silver somewhere in a mountain cave, waiting to be found.

The Niagara Falls and Grand Canyon of the South: Cumberland Falls and Cumberland Gap

And both are located right here in Kentucky! There are two Niagara Falls—one in the North in New York/Ontario and one in the South in Kentucky. Ours is better.

Located in Daniel Boone National Forest, Cumberland Falls plunges more than 125 feet to a rock-lined bed. The falls are also more than sixty feet wide. This all sounds like pretty standard falls stuff, not much different than Niagara. Here's why Cumberland Falls is better: Kentucky's Cumberland Falls is home to the only predictable moonbow—a lunar rainbow—in the Western Hemisphere. The moonbow is a natural phenomenon of a beam of light, from the moon of course, that shoots across the falls. It is visible in the mist of the falls and can be viewed only on a clear night lit by a full moon.

Take that, Niagara!

While Cumberland Falls is considered the Niagara of the South, Cumberland Gap is the Grand Canyon of the South—the only break in the Cumberland Mountains and a famous exploring path.

The first records of the Gap are from surveyor Dr. Thomas Walker in 1750. Walker's fame came not from exploring the Gap but from his relationship to Thomas Jefferson. Walker was the doctor for Jefferson's father, Peter. When Peter died, Walker was entrusted as young Jefferson's guardian. After being bitten by the surveying and exploring bug, Walker left medicine behind and plunged ahead to the Gap. His journal entries of what he saw on April 13, 1750, are the first known recordings of the Cumberland Gap.

Of course Walker wasn't the first person to find the Gap. Archeologists believe that animals used the Gap in prehistoric times for migratory purposes. Native Americans, too, are thought to have

Home of the moonbow.

taken advantage of the Gap's geographical location, as the Gap borders three states that were known for their natural bounty: Tennessee, Virginia, and Kentucky.

Due to its location, the Gap served as a coveted position during the Civil War, and over the course of the war it exchanged hands more than ten times. In 1861 the Confederates seized the Gap, only to abandon it in 1862. After that, Gen. George W. Morgan of the Union took control. The Confederates returned and kicked the Union soldiers out. On September 7, 1863, Maj. Gen. Ambrose Burnside of the Union took control yet again of the Gap for a final time. In 1864 Ulysses S. Grant declared the Gap the "Gibraltar of America!"

In June of 1940 Cumberland Gap became the largest historical park in the country, with more than 20,000 acres of land.

Cumberland Falls State Resort Park is located at 7351 Highway 90 in Corbin. For information call (606) 528-4121. For information about Cumberland Gap National Historical Park, call (606) 248-2817 or visit www.nps.gov/cuga.

The "Shortest" US President

You probably didn't read about him in history class. That's because he's conveniently missing from most history texts. But the shortest US president—in length of service, that is—David Rice Atchison, was from Frogtown.

Atchison, president pro tem of the Senate, served a mere twenty-four hours when James K. Polk's term expired and the very religious Zachary Taylor refused to take office on a Sunday. It happened on March 4, 1849. Polk left office at midnight. Taylor refused to take office on March 4 because it was a Sunday, so Atchison was president for a day—the most uneventful presidency in US history.

Atchison himself didn't consider it a major achievement. In fact when asked what he did during his one day as the nation's chief executive, he told a reporter he slept most of it. "I went to bed. There had been two or three busy nights finishing up the work of the Senate, and I slept most of that Sunday." His hometown of Frogtown has since been renamed Kirklevington for obvious reasons. Who would want a president from Frogtown?

Dog Patch Trading Post
London

You need to be of a certain age to understand the name of this souvenir stand. Otherwise, it's just a funny name. But if you were a comic page reader before 1977, you know that Dogpatch was the fictional home of the wildly popular Li'l Abner.

Abner Yokum, his girlfriend Daisy Mae, and their assorted friends, family, and neighbors were the Dukes of Hazzard long before there was a *Dukes of Hazzard*.

★ ★

Connecticut-born cartoonist Al Capp started his hillbilly comic strip in 1934, and within a few years it had attracted more than 60 million readers. He based his creation on stereotypes, in particular stereotypes of Kentucky hillbillies.

Capp originally set the strip in Kentucky. A panel in the ninth strip referred to "Dogpatch, Kentucky," a reference he repeated two years later when he had Li'l Abner buy a train ticket to "Dogpatch, Kain-tucky." But he soon dropped the specific Kentucky reference and made Dogpatch a generic southern hillbilly community.

In Kentucky we didn't take offense to Capp's stereotypes. We were proud to be part of this national sensation. Proud enough to name a souvenir shop after it. The Dog Patch Trading Post opened in the spring of 1950. It was originally on US Highway 25 but later relocated next to the interstate and expanded to its current strip center location.

Today, the store is your one-stop shop for "remote control fart machines" ($15.98), "hillbilly hats" ($6.98), and "Mother's cedar boxes" inscribed with "A mother's heart is like a rose, always open, always loving" ($24.98).

The Dog Patch Trading Post, Kentucky's oldest and largest souvenir shop, is located at exit 41 on Interstate 75 near London. Call (606) 864-4531 or check out the website at www.dogpatchtradingpost.com.

Shake a Tail Feather

London

When it comes to chicken, the folks of Laurel County do chicken right. And well they should, because the place was home to Colonel Harland Sanders's first restaurant and also the first restaurant of Lee Cummings, the Colonel's nephew and the cofounder of Lee's Famous Recipe Chicken.

So each September they drag out the World's Largest Stainless Steel Skillet, fry up a mess of chicken, and pay tribute to this heritage with their annual eggs-travaganza, the World Chicken Festival. The skillet is 10.5 feet in diameter and eight inches deep with an eight-foot handle.

It would not work for a pancake festival because it weighs seven hundred pounds and would require several Arnold Schwarzeneggers to flip. The skillet can hold three hundred gallons of cooking oil and can cook six hundred quarters of chicken at a time.

A quarter-million people are "eggs-pected" each fall for the four-day event. They are filled with "eggs-citement"—and also filled with chicken. More than 30,000 fried chicken dinners have been fried up in the giant skillet. They serve up more fried chicken than anywhere else in the world during the festival—and also make more uses of the word "eggs" in puns than you thought could "eggs-ist."

For information call (800) 348-0095 or visit www.chickenfestival.com.

You'll have an eggs-cellent time at the World Chicken Festival.
LONDON-LAUREL COUNTY TOURIST COMMISSION

Camp Wildcat

Camp Wildcat isn't a summer basketball camp for middle school boys who worship the University of Kentucky's Wildcats.

It was a Civil War battlefield, a site that might more accurately be called the Battle That Never Was.

Kentucky never seceded from the Union and had split loyalties during the war. That made the state a battleground, with each side seeking to gain control. In September 1861 a Union force began gathering at a ridge overlooking the Rockcastle River on the Old Wilderness Road, the main north-south road in eastern Kentucky at the time.

Confederate soldiers were invading through the Cumberland Gap and had already routed a Union group at the Cumberland Ford near Pineville. But by the time the rebels reached the river in late October, the Union reinforcements had arrived at what was now called Camp Wildcat.

The Confederates made two unsuccessful parries then retreated. *The Cincinnati Gazette* reported the southern attack "was unsuccessful simply because it came twenty-four hours too late."

The battle, such as it was, was over. All told, four Union soldiers died and eighteen were injured while the Confederates lost eleven men with another forty-two wounded.

The U.S.D.A. Forest Service notes, "Camp Wildcat wasn't one of the great battles of the Civil War." But it was the first time regular troops were engaged in Kentucky during the war. And as such it was a harbinger of things to come.

Kentucky never fell to the South.

Camp Wildcat is located in Laurel County, about eight miles north of London in tiny Hazel Patchoff. Take exit 49 from Interstate 75 and head east on State Road 900 for 0.6 miles on 909, then head south on US Highway 25. Continue 0.7 miles before turning left on Hazel Patch Road. From there, follow the signs. *Caution:* This last road is a gravel road that may not be passable by vehicles with low clearance.

For more information visit the website at www.campwildcat preservationfoundation.org.

Country Music Highway

Maybe Kentucky doesn't have the musical reputation of, say, Tennessee or Texas, but it can hold its own with either of those states when it comes to homegrown musical talent, particularly in the field of country music.

To recognize this—or more precisely, to get the rest of the nation to recognize this—in 2002 Kentucky's Tourism Department created the Country Music Highway.

Sure, it's a tourism invention, but it's a neat little trip—144 miles of gawking at the landscape that gave America such talents as the Judds, Billy Ray Cyrus (he of the wonderful mullet haircut), Loretta Lynn, Dwight Yoakam, Tom T. Hall, and Ricky Skaggs.

The state claims that the highway—technically it's US Highway 23—has produced more country music stars than any similar stretch of highway in the US. And I have no evidence to the contrary.

The highway runs through eight counties in eastern Kentucky, from the Virginia state line on the south to the Ohio border on the north. There's even a Country Music Highway Museum in Paintsville, featuring memorabilia from Country Music Highway stars.

Among the highway's highlights:

The Billie Jean Osborne's Kentucky Opry—a year-round show featuring country, bluegrass, and gospel.

Ashland's Paramount Arts Center—the restored Depression-era art deco movie theater where Billy Ray Cyrus filmed the video for his hit, "Achy Breaky Heart."

Butcher Hollow, south of Paintsville—the hometown of Loretta Lynn and Crystal Gayle. When you arrive at the house, honk, and Herman, Loretta's brother, will give you a guided tour of the small frame home.

For more information on the Country Music Highway—US Highway 23—visit the website at www.countrymusichighway.com.

* *

Jailbird Judge

Louisa

In addition to being the birthplace of the Hanging Judge, Judge Roy Bean (born in Mason County in 1825), Kentucky is also the home state of Frederick Vinson, the only chief justice of the United States Supreme Court born in jail.

That's right: the only chief justice of the United States Supreme Court born in jail—not that any other chief justices have clamored to argue the distinction. But Vinson was proud of the fact and famously amused the Washington cocktail set with his boast.

How did it happen? When Vinson was born in 1890, his father was the jailer in Louisa. The family lived in an apartment in the jail, and that's where Vinson was born.

Vinson also holds the distinction of never missing a Centre College football game—even though he has been dead since 1953. Brothers of his old fraternity, Phi Delta Theta, adopted the habit of taking his portrait—affectionately dubbed Dead Fred—to home football and basketball games, and he's been in attendance at every game for the last four decades.

Little Bang Theory

Middlesboro

It was long before CNN and Fox News so there wasn't much coverage. In fact there was *no* coverage when a giant meteor a quarter-mile in diameter crashed down in southeastern Kentucky 300 million years ago, creating a crater some four miles wide. Daniel Boone was several million years from crossing into Kentucky through the Cumberland Gap. But jump ahead to, oh, 1889, and watch as the Middlesborough Town Company, an English corporation, buys land in the Cumberland Gap area and founds the town of Middlesborough, better known today as Middlesboro.

The site they picked for their city was in the heart of the meteor crater, though they didn't know it. But their astute judgment makes Middlesboro the only city in the US built in a meteor crater.

Homegrown Hustler

Scratch the surface of First Amendment champion Larry Flynt and you'll find a hustler at heart. That's how he grew up in the backwoods of northern Kentucky—and that's how he made his name: hustling a lowbrow porn magazine named *Hustler*.

Flynt grew up dirt poor in dirt-poor Magoffin County. "The biggest industry was jury duty," he once told the *Louisville Courier-Journal*.

In 1958 sixteen-year-old Flynt used his 1951 Ford to run bootleg whiskey around the county. He made his name in the skin trade after moving to Dayton, Ohio, and opening a strip club in 1965. The first Hustler Club opened there in 1968. The magazine named for the club debuted in 1974 to underwhelming reviews (another magazine called it the most boring publication in America except for *Refrigerator Monthly*).

The magazine was headed for oblivion until Flynt bought nude photos of Jacqueline Kennedy Onassis from a spy photographer in 1975 for $18,000. And thus the modern *Hustler* was born.

Cross My Heart
Middlesboro

Harrison Mayes had a vision. While pinned against the wall of a Kentucky coalmine by a runaway coal car, the life being squeezed from him, he saw a cross. But not just any cross—a giant cross. "I said, Lord if you'll let me live, I'll build it," Mayes told me in 1980, seven years before his death.

And build it he did—a large cross of light bulbs on the mountain overlooking Middlesboro's east side. But he didn't stop there. He built

The old, rugged concrete cross.

★ ★

a concrete mold and began pouring cement crosses, hundreds of them, which he transported all over the country, erecting these road-side religious monuments warning JESUS IS COMING SOON AND PREPARE TO MEET GOD all over the southern US. If you drove to Florida on vacation in the years before interstates, you probably saw one of his crosses.

But he didn't stop there, either. He built a new home in the shape of a cross. Mayes told me he once had a cross-shaped sign out front of his house that read IF YOU GO TO HELL IT'S YOUR OWN FAULT. The neighbors complained so much he finally took it down.

Many of the crosses have crumbled or been bulldozed for highway expansion. But his cross-shaped house remains, a monument to one man's obsession with a religious symbol. It's at 409 Chester Avenue, which runs off the main drag in downtown, Highway 74 West. The home is still a private residence.

First Commercial Oil Well

The nation's first commercial oil well was a mistake. Located in McCreary County, the well was originally drilled in search of brine used by salt makers. However, once drilling began in 1818, they found that they had struck gold. The well, known as the Martin Beatty Well, produced large quantities of oil.

Kentucky's production of oil didn't stop there. The people of Exxon got involved and have the record for the deepest oil well—the Exxon No. 1 Duncan in Webster County—at a depth of 15,200 feet. Henderson County holds the state record for the most oil produced at 109 million barrels.

Fore!

Middlesboro

Want to see how golf was played a hundred years ago without having to charter a flight to Scotland? Then visit the Middlesboro Country Club, which claims to be "the oldest continuously played golf course in the United States."

The golf club was founded in 1889 by a group of English investors who had immigrated to the Cumberland Gap region. They founded the town, laying out wide English-style streets and building Tudor homes. But they sorely missed their beloved game of golf. After scouting the area a bit, they discovered the Yellow Creek Valley and deemed it a suitable place to build a golf course.

Middlesboro Country Club retains its original layout, and that includes the majestic oaks that were lining the fairways when the club was built over a century ago. It's only a nine-hole course, but in 1889 it was quite an undertaking to build.

There are older golf clubs in the country. The Country Club of Charleston (South Carolina), for instance, was founded in 1786. But all the others closed for long periods of time. There is no older club where golf has been played continuously.

Middlesboro Country Club is a private club, but it welcomes visitors. For information call (606) 248-3831.

The Hundred-Million-Dollar Hole

Middlesboro

It's an impressive hole, drilled straight through Cumberland Mountain. But it's still just a hole.

The hole has a name—the Cumberland Gap Tunnel—and there is no question that it is a marvel of modern engineering technology. It cost $280 million and took seventeen years to burrow the one-mile hole through the hill. The nickname, the Hundred Million Dollar Hole, comes from the early years of the project. That was the initial projection of how much it would cost. Someone forgot to figure in cost overruns.

★ ★

The Cumberland Gap Tunnel opened in 1996 and carries US Highway 25 East from Kentucky to Tennessee and Virginia. It replaced a road that followed the old Wilderness Trail through Cumberland Gap, meaning that old road meandered up the hill taking the same course a cow would. As one of the most deadly stretches of highway in the country, it had to be replaced. An average of one death occurred there every month, and locals called it "Massacre Mountain."

The tunnel did the deed. There hasn't been a fatality along this stretch of road since it opened, even though traffic on the highway has doubled. The local congressman, Hal Rogers, calls it "the most significant thing that has happened here since Daniel Boone began to bring settlers through the Gap." He's right.

The Cumberland Gap Tunnel is on US Highway 25 East between Middlesboro and Cumberland Gap.

Mullet
Head

It's the haircut of a thousand names: Tennessee Top Hat (because of its popularity among country music fans), the Mississippi Mudflap (because that's what it looks like), the Ape Drape, the Soccer Rocker, and Hockey Hair. It's even been called the Kentucky Waterfall (for the precipitous drop the locks make). Hairdressers call it the Bi-Level. Barbers call it by its most common appellation: the Mullet. It's the male haircut that's short in front and long in back. And it's most famous devotee has been Flatwoods, Kentucky, native Billy Ray Cyrus, the country music star famous for his hit records "Some Gave All," "Trail of Tears," and "Achy Breaky Heart." That last hit has given the Mullet yet another name. People who don't like the haircut have been known to call it the Achy-Breaky-Mistake-y!

Why the South Lost the War

Nancy

Felix Zollicoffer was a newspaperman by trade but when the Civil War broke out he was named a brigadier general in the Provisional Army of Tennessee. What?

That was probably the last time a newspaperman was ever given command of a fighting force.

General Zollicoffer led his men—5,400 strong!—through the Cumberland Gap with orders to take eastern Kentucky.

And they did, winning the Battle of Barbourville, the first Confederate victory in the state of Kentucky.

Unfortunately for Zollicoffer the war went on.

Tombs of the Unfortunate Soldiers.

★ ★

He was ordered to take his men to Mill Springs and prepare to defend the area. He had a choice of two defensive positions: the southern bank of the Cumberland River, which featured a bluff, or the northern bank, which was low and flat.

He was a newspaperman, not a military strategist, and he chose the weakest defensive position, the north bank.

His men were routed in the subsequent Battle of Mill Springs. Zollicoffer, who was nearsighted, wandered into the nearby Union camp by mistake, thinking he spotted rebel soldiers, and was shot. The old newspaperman had met his deadline.

The Mill Springs Battlefield is located at 9020 West Highway 80 in Nancy, just outside Somerset. For more information check out the website at www.millsprings.net.

Big, Scary, and Square

It was a hot July night in 1986, and Mary Helton was finishing up at her Countryside Restaurant in Oneida. Suddenly a large object loomed in the sky over Bullskin Mountain. "It was very big, scary, and square with windows," she would later tell the *Manchester Enterprise*. If Helton were the only one to observe the big, scary, and square UFO, it would be easy to discount. But scores of other people in the area called the local newspaper, airport, and weather station.

Air traffic controllers at the London airport insisted it must have been a B-52 flying low overhead, but locals insisted they had seen airplanes—and this was no airplane. It was flying too low and too slow.

The newspaper investigated, but no explanation was ever found. The good news is that the big, scary, square object has never returned.

* *

Home of the Feuding McCoys

Pikeville

Let's take a trip down to Pike County, Kentucky, to play a game of family feud.

The feud between the West Virginia Hatfields and Kentucky McCoys is perhaps the longest and best-known family rivalry. The rivalry has outlasted the original family descendants, been intertwined through marriages, and claimed the lives of thirteen persons and one pig. In fact, a pig is what started the whole ordeal.

The Hatfields and McCoys were very much patriarchal families, run by the men of the house, which was the custom of the time and the mountain region. Randolph "Ole Ran'l" McCoy was not known for his charm. He was often described by members of his own clan as "mean" and "grumpy." Ole Ran'l and his wife, Sarah, who also happened to be his cousin, had a total of fifteen children—nine boys and six girls.

Captain William Anderson "Devil Anse" Hatfield was the mirror image of Ole Ran'l. Devil Anse was known for his charm, wit, and, most of all, his humor. With his wife, Levicy, Devil Anse had thirteen children—nine boys and four girls.

A game of sorts developed between the two families, members of whom snuck over the border to steal each other's pigs and horses. This game of thievery never amounted to more than a slight inconvenience for both families.

While the game of "they stole my pig" never really made any waves, Ole Ran'l had had enough in the fall of 1878. Ole Ran'l had gone to visit a Kentucky Hatfield who had married his sister when he spotted a pig that looked familiar to him (no one quite knows exactly how Ole Ran'l "knew'" the pig so to speak, but he did). Ole Ran'l told his brother-in-law Floyd that the pig was his and accused him of stealing from kin, a grave sin. Floyd denied all accusations of theft and said that the pig had always been his. Ole Ran'l took Floyd to court to settle the matter once and for all.

Anse Hatfield served as judge over the case, and the jury consisted of six McCoys and six Hatfields. The entire case hinged on the testimony of Bill Staton, who swore that Floyd rightfully owned the pig. Staton just happened to be the brother-in-law of Ellison Hatfield, who was Devil Anse's brother. Floyd won the case.

Ole Ran'l was furious at the outcome, so much so that he put a hit out on Staton and the pig. Shortly after the trial, Staton was shot by Paris and Sam McCoy. Sam stood trial for the murder but was acquitted because Devil Anse got involved and persuaded the jury to find him not guilty as a sign of truce between the two families. The gesture was lost on Ole Ran'l, who felt that Sam should not have had to go to trial in the first place. War between the two clans was declared. The feud and killing went back and forth until it finally came to an end in 1891. The final death toll was thirteen—plus the pig.

Both patriarchs lived long lives, well into their eighties. Ole Ran'l died March 28, 1941. Devil Anse became a born-again Christian and died January 6, 1921, from pneumonia. Ole Ran'l McCoy is buried in the Dils Cemetery at US Highway 460 and Old US 23 Bypass. For information call (800) 844-7453.

More Fun Than a Barrel of Moonshine
Pikeville

Pikeville, the county seat of Pike County, Kentucky, is home to the most notable hillbillies of all time, the McCoys. It's also home to the Hillbilly Days Festival.

Organized by Howard "Dirty Ear" Stratton and "Shady" Grady Kinney, the festival began in 1977 as an effort to raise money for the Shriners children's hospitals and burn centers. Mountain clans from all over the nation turned out for the "family reunion."

Every year downtown Pikeville is transformed into an outdoor festival, complete with a dance floor for the clogging and square dance competitions. Mountain music permeates the area, and children and adults of all ages participate in the hillbilly costume contest.

Hillbilly Days are held every April. For information call (800) 844-7453 or visit www.hillbillydays.com.

P Is for Pepsi; P Is for Pikeville

There are some curiosities for which there is no explanation. This is one of them. Pikeville annually leads the nation in per capita consumption of Pepsi Cola. It's not a recent phenomenon. It's a long-standing love affair by a town for a drink. Pepsi wasn't invented here (it was created in North Carolina), and there's no known connection. People in Pikeville just prefer Pepsi. (Try saying that five times real fast.)

Even a 2001 commemorative Coke bottle celebrating the town's Hillbilly Days Festival didn't change the equation. Coke sold out of the bottle with the hillbilly on it, but Pepsi remained number one in local supermarkets.

Bridging the Gap

Slade

The Natural Bridge is a rock that goes from one hill to another. Yep, a rock. It measures seventy-eight feet long and sixty-five feet high—yet most people never know they're on it.

To get to the bridge you can take a lift or torture yourself with stair climbing. Once you get to the top there are no markers, no large arrows pointing to it, no sign that says YOU'RE ON IT. When most people get to the bridge, they are impressed with the scenery and large drop-off on both sides. But they rarely recognize that they wouldn't be able to see the beauty around them if they weren't standing on, say it with me, a bridge.

The bridge cloaks itself in the surrounding area, hence the term "natural."

★ ★

So when you go to see the Natural Bridge and you find yourself standing high in the hills, taking in the bountiful scenery and wondering where this bridge that you've come so far to see is, look down. You're on it.

The Natural Bridge is in the Daniel Boone National Forest. From the Mountain Parkway, take Highway 11 to Natural Bridge State Park. For information call (606) 663-2214 or visit http://parks.ky.gov/parks/resortparks/natural-bridge/default.aspx.

Rest for the Weary Shoeshine Man
Slade

Not many shoeshine men have a rest area named after them. Then again, not many shoeshine men *lobby* to have one named after them. Junior Williamson, a native of Pike County, was a shoeshine man at the Capitol in Frankfort. Every day he diligently shined the shoes of the state's top politicians. He was known for his humanitarian endeavors, volunteer works, and general all-around good-guy demeanor. Everyone loved Junior.

Junior felt that a rest area was needed near the Slade/Beattyville exit. This particular location was important as it served as the main entrance to the Natural Bridge State Park. So Junior lobbied the politicians each day for its construction as he shined their shoes. And while he was polishing the shoes, he also polished the proverbial apple, suggesting they could even name it after him.

The Junior Williamson Rest Area is near exit 33 on the Mountain Parkway.

Quintessential Kentuckians
Ashley Judd

If you didn't know better, you'd think there is a typo on Ashley Judd's resume: "Born in Los Angeles."

Ashley Judd, the University of Kentucky basketball team's number one fan. Ashley Judd, the non-singing daughter and little sister of Kentucky's famous country duo, The Judds. Ashley Judd, Ashland Paul Blazer High School's most famous alum.

That Ashley Judd was born in Los Angeles?

Judd considers her birth "an accident." She is, she proudly notes, an "eighth-generation Kentuckian." The fact that she was born in Los Angeles—well, her parents just happened to be living there when her mother, country singer Naomi Judd, gave birth to her youngest daughter.

Acting might seem like a strange career choice for Judd. Her mom and sister are singers. She studied French. "I didn't do anything like acting as a kid. I had one directing class in college and I think I had to act in someone else's scene. But I never did anything serious."

She almost didn't try it. "I was six weeks away from leaving for the Peace Corps when I said I have to trust God and try this. I got a U-Haul with 'Cecil B. DeMille Here I Come,' and it was Hollywood or bust."

And she hasn't looked back. From her first role, a small part in the Christian Slater movie *Kuff*, to starring turns in *Ruby in Paradise, Heat, Smoke, A Time to Kill,* and *Kiss the Girls,* among others, Ashley Judd went from "Naomi's girl" and "Wynonna's little sister" to Ashley Judd, actress.

And Ashley Judd, the University of Kentucky's number one basketball fan. When the TV cameras scan the U.K. crowd at a basketball game and settle on Ashley Judd in her gray Kentucky T-shirt, the block letters *Kentucky* stand for more than just a university. They represent the state of Ashley's soul. "Quite frankly I don't think I would be as tender and soulful if I weren't from Kentucky.

★ ★

Where They Milk More Snakes Than Any Other Place in the World
Slade

To most visitors the Kentucky Reptile Zoo is just another tourist attraction—"Would you mind posing with one of your distant relatives, Mildred? Ha-ha." But it's also the world's largest supplier of snake venom for medical research. Malayan pit viper venom, for instance, is used in research on drugs to treat stroke victims and sells for about $50 a gram. Sounds like easy money—until you find out it takes about twenty-five snakes to produce about a gram of venom. Easy money if you don't mind "milking" a snake. How do you milk a snake? You'll have to come watch. That's another attraction at the Kentucky Reptile Zoo. Snake milking happens about every two weeks, so call ahead to coordinate your schedule.

The Kentucky Reptile Zoo is located behind the Mountain Parkway's Junior Williamson Rest Area on Highway 11. Call (606) 663-9160 or visit online at www.kyreptilezoo.org.

Cruisin' Capital
Somerset

Kentucky has an Official State Bird (cardinal) and an Official Agricultural Insect (honeybee) and an Official Drink (milk). You probably thought the Official Drink was Bourbon. Surprise.

But who would have thought that Kentucky had an Official Car Cruise Capital?

Unless you have driven through Somerset—or read the small print in the newspaper—you probably wouldn't have known.

In 2011, Kentucky Governor Steve Beshear signed a resolution proclaiming Somerset as the "Official Car Cruise Capital of Kentucky."

What's a car cruise you may be asking? It's when men of a certain age drag that old car they've been restoring out of the garage, polish it up, and take it downtown, to drive up and down the main drag endlessly.

It happens in cities all over the country. But only Kentucky has an Official Car Cruise Capital.

The designation is in recognition of Somerset's success with its Somernites Cruise series. Every fourth Saturday from April through October old car enthusiasts bring their vintage automobiles to downtown Somerset to "cruise the Strip," the Strip being the downtown section of US Highway 27.

Each weekend show will average more than a thousand old cars. The population of Somerset is only 12,000.

The Town Square is at the intersection of Main (KY Highway 1247) and Mt. Vernon Road (KY Highway 80). For more information check out the website at www.somernitescruise.com.

Still a Union Stronghold
Vanceburg

Vanceburg is home to the only freestanding monument dedicated to the Union soldiers who fought in the Civil War. This may seem risky for a small, southern town in a state that supported slavery, but diversity is something Vanceburg was founded on.

Vanceburg was settled in 1797 by Moses Baird, who led a group of men to Kentucky in search of riches in the salt-making industry. Baird liked the area he settled in so much that he named it Vanceburg after a friend, Joseph Vance. While much of the state relied upon slave labor to work the crops, and thus many supported the Confederates, 107 Vanceburg men died in the war efforts as Union soldiers. A monument was erected in 1884 in their honor. The monument is listed with the National Register of Historic Places as the only Union monument south of the Mason-Dixon Line.

Inscribed on the monument is this: "The war for the Union was right, everlastingly right, and the war against the Union was wrong, forever wrong." Then follows the list of the 107 Lewis County Union men killed during the war.

The monument is on the courthouse lawn on Second Street.

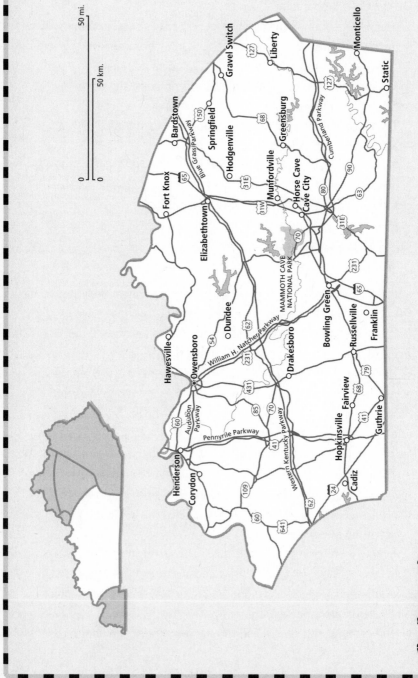

The Pennyrile

4

The Pennyrile

I wish there *were a better story for why the south-central part of the state from the Tennessee River to the Appalachian Mountains is known as the Pennyrile. The name is just the way Kentuckians pronounce, or mispronounce, pennyroyal.*

What's a pennyroyal, you ask? From the name you might think that kings and paupers converged to settle the frontiers of south-central Kentucky. And you would be wrong. Actually, pennyroyal is a mint-like plant that was once as ubiquitous to the area as kudzu is now. Even the name pennyroyal is a corruption; the proper name, the name herbalists use, is Pulioll-royall. *Pliny (the Elder, I believe) gave the plant its name.* Pulex *is Latin for fleas, and Pliny noted how marvelous the plant was at driving the pesky bugs away.*

In modern times the main use for pennyroyal has been in an herbal tea that is reputed to relieve gas. The green leaves of the plant are also held in high esteem by bunny breeders because the leaves reduce diarrhea in their rabbits.

I would be willing to bet that most of the people who live in the Pennyrile are unfamiliar with these stories. But it does explain the preponderance of curious stories in the area.

★ ★

Counter Culture

Bardstown

Hurst Drugs in Bardstown is a throwback to the old days, when the drugstore was more than just a place to get a prescription filled. Part of the charm of drugstores in the old days was the soda fountain. Soda fountains weren't just for lunch. They were for breakfast and midmorning coffee; they were for afternoon smokes and after-school cokes. At the end of World War II, 60 percent of America's drugstores had working soda fountains, according to a 1948 edition of *Remington's Practice of Pharmacy.* Not anymore. You have to drive a long way nowadays to find a drugstore soda fountain, but we still have a few in Kentucky. There's Wagner's Pharmacy on Fourth Street in

Belly up for the best ice-cream soda you've ever had.

Louisville, a favorite with the jockeys and trainers at nearby Churchill Downs. Smith Pharmacy in Burkesville, the state's oldest drugstore, still operates a soda fountain. At Hutchinson Drug Store in Lexington's Victorian Square, they still make ice cream sodas the old-fashioned way.

On my most recent visit to Hurst Drugs, Pat the counter lady fixed me the most perfect grilled-cheese sandwich, with the corners seared, and a vanilla milk shake that made me forswear ever buying another drive-thru shake.

Hurst Drugs is located at 102 North Third Street in Bardstown (502-348-9261). The food's good, the service is great, and the friendly customers are tops.

Bourbon Invented by Baptist Minister!

Bardstown

Oscar Getz didn't invent Bourbon. That is generally credited to Elijah Craig—and we thank him for it—a Baptist minister who operated a still in Georgetown, Kentucky, a town that is now dry (alcoholic beverages prohibited), in the 1780s. But isn't that a nifty tabloid headline: Bourbon Invented by Baptist Minister! If only it were true.

But Oscar Getz did invent the Whiskey Museum, sort of. It's called the Oscar Getz Museum of Whiskey History, and it's in the Bourbon Capital of the World, Bardstown, which was at one time home to twenty-two distilleries. For decades whiskey distilling was the town's only industry. They've branched out now, into tourism. That's where the Oscar Getz Museum of Whiskey History comes in.

It's there that you can hear the story of Elijah Craig, reputed inventor of bourbon whiskey. Alexis Lichine's *New Encyclopedia of Wines & Spirits* says, "Early in the colonial history of America, a Baptist minister, Elijah Craig, established a still in Georgetown, Kentucky, and began producing whiskey from a base of corn. The still is said to have been one of the first in Kentucky, and customers in neighboring towns christened his product Bourbon County Whiskey, from the county of origin."

It's a great story—they even teach it in Kentucky schools—but it isn't true.

There *was* an Elijah Craig, and he *did* distill whiskey. But he didn't do it in Bourbon County. He never lived in Bourbon County. And he wasn't alone as a distiller of spirits; it was a fact of life in pioneer days. The claim for Craig wasn't even made until a century later in Richard Collins's *History of Kentucky,* published in 1874. The first bourbon was most likely distilled in the first Kentucky settlement: Fort Harrod (now Harrodsburg), which was established in 1774. Bourbon County wasn't even established for another fifteen years, and then it was named for the reigning royal family of France, the Bourbons.

At that time Bourbon County was the size of thirty-four modern counties. As the legislature carved out more and more counties, the region came to be known as Old Bourbon. So when whiskey was shipped downriver to other areas, it became known as Old Bourbon Whiskey. It was soon recognized as the best—we Kentuckians are good with vices. Customers began demanding Bourbon whiskey. Other whiskey makers latched onto the name and, voila, bourbon whiskey was born.

You can hear that story and see enough whiskey bottles to decorate a freshman dorm at the Oscar Getz Museum of Whiskey History. And find out about Oscar Getz, who didn't invent bourbon whiskey, either, but was a great student of the brand. His family owned the old Tom Moore Distillery in Bardstown, and Getz developed a taste for his subject, studying whiskey's history and collecting anything and everything bourbon related. He lectured on the subject in the 1950s and '60s, and after his death in 1983 his widow donated his collection to the city of Bardstown, which opened it to the world in this museum of whiskey.

Sorry, no free samples.

The Oscar Getz Museum of Whiskey History is in Spalding Hall at 114 North Fifth Street. For information call (502) 348-2999 or visit the website at www.whiskeymuseum.com.

Come on in and meet the vice squad.

Lucky 13 House
Bardstown

Federal Hill, Judge John Rowan's Plantation House in Bardstown, takes the number 13 to an extreme. There are thirteen windows, thirteen-inch-thick walls, thirteen steps in each of the four staircases, thirteen mantels, thirteen railings on each landing, thirteen earthquake-protection bars, and thirteen-foot-high ceilings. That's because Rowan, who was everything from Kentucky secretary of state to United States senator, believed 13 was a lucky number.

★ ★

It has been for some who've stayed there—Stephen Foster, for example. Legend has it that Foster stayed here in 1828 while visiting his cousins, the rowdy Rowan kids. The legend also has it that he composed "My Old Kentucky Home" at the Rowan family piano and wrote it down at the family desk. Good legends, but no one can prove them.

The house hasn't been as lucky for others, including the sixteen persons who died from cholera here in 1833.

If you're an aspiring songwriter, interested in penning state anthems (Foster wrote Kentucky's and Florida's), by all means check it out. Thirteen could be lucky for you. If you believe otherwise, don't go.

Federal Hill is now part of My Old Kentucky Home State Park, located in Bardstown at 501 East Stephen Foster Avenue. For tour information call (502) 348-3502 or visit online at http://parks.ky.gov/parks/recreationparks/old-ky-home/default.aspx.

The Haunted Nelson County Jail
Bardstown

From 1797 until it was decommissioned in 1987, almost two hundred years later, the Nelson County Jail housed prisoners. At the time it closed, it was the oldest operating jail in Kentucky.

Its most famous prisoner was the "wicked" Martin Hill, a prisoner at the jail in 1885, who was sentenced to be hanged for the murder of his wife. However, a terrible illness overcame Hill and he was never executed. In his last days, Hill was in extreme pain. His loud screams and delirious rants echoed throughout the dungeon. At that time there were only two cells and an upstairs prisoner's dungeon. The most dangerous of the criminals were shackled to the floor in the dungeon. Inmates claimed they could hear Hill's violent screams even after his death.

Of course, the old Nelson County Jail is now the Jailer's Inn Bed and Breakfast. It was opened just two years after the prison was shut down. If you couldn't already tell where this was going, Jailer's Inn is on the Travel Channel's list of ten most haunted places in America.

Jailhouse of rock.

Many sightings and sounds of ghosts have been reported over the years, from guests, tour guides, and visitors. They report hearing everything from high-pitched screams to the cries of a baby to actual sightings of men in the rooms.

There's no extra charge if you see a ghost.

The Jailer's Inn is located at 111 W. Stephen Foster Avenue in Bardstown. For more information check out the website at www.jailers inn.com.

Everything Including the Kitchen Sink
Bowling Green

What is the largest flea market in Kentucky? That's easy. It's Flea Land.

Here's the catch: *Which* Flea Land?

The Flea Land in London calls itself "Kentucky's Largest Flea Market" on its billboards on Interstate 75, with 80,000 square feet of Beanie Babies and other assorted flea-market favorites. But the fact is, the state's largest flea market is its sister site, Flea Land in Bowling Green, with 85,000 square feet of booths and merchandise.

Flea Land of Bowling Green is five buildings connected by hallways and cigarette stench. If you're allergic to smoke, you might want to avoid this curiosity.

Flea Land of Bowling Green is located off exit 22 on Interstate 65 at 1100 Three Springs Road. It is open Saturday and Sunday 9:00 a.m. to 6:00 p.m. Adjoining Flea Land is the Antique Mall at Flea Land, which is open daily 10:00 a.m. to 5:00 p.m.

Flea Land of London, which boasts more than 500 booths, is still pretty big, even if it is 5,000 square feet smaller than Flea Land of Bowling Green. It is located off Interstate 75 at exit 38 on Highway 229, at the Highway 192 Bypass. Call (270) 843-1978 or visit www .flealand.com.

The Steamboat Blues

John Fitch wasn't born in Kentucky—he was born in Connecticut in 1743—but he died here. Fitch had a tough childhood and an unhappy marriage. But he also had a dream, and in 1782 he moved to Pennsylvania with a grand scheme: to build a steamboat.

He was able to secure financial backing from private investors to pursue his newfound obsession. In 1790 Fitch completed the first successful steamboat passenger run between Philadelphia and Trenton, New Jersey. No one paid too much attention to the fact that the boat could only reach speeds of six to eight miles per hour. Instead most people laughed at the design. Resembling a long canoe, the steamboat had six oars on each side, powered by a steam engine. Those who did not laugh at the contraption feared it. They were scared that stepping foot aboard Fitch's steamboat would be the last step they took. Needless to say, it was a hard sell to the public. Fitch went back to the drawing board and replaced the oars with giant paddles. It didn't work— and it still scared the masses.

Fitch eventually called it quits and fled to Bardstown for the sole purpose of killing himself. Fitch made a deal with the local innkeeper: For an exchange of 150 acres of land, the innkeeper agreed to house Fitch and give him one pint of whiskey a day. Drinking himself to death didn't work, so Fitch gave the inn- keeper another 150 acres of land and upped the ante to two pints of whiskey a day. It still didn't work. Fitch was a failure at suicide. Not wanting to waste any more time—plus he had run out of land to give away—Fitch finally overdosed on opium in his Bardstown room.

★ ★

More Than a Cake Mix
Bowling Green

Duncan Hines was the Zagat of his time. A printing salesman by trade, he roamed the country, taste-testing roadside diners from Maine to Miami, from the Atlantic to the Pacific. He first collected his comments in a handy-dandy foldout guide, which he included with his Christmas cards in 1934. His friends and family were so appreciative that he began publishing a regular guide, which he called *Adventures in Good Eating.* Each year it got bigger and fatter—and more popular.

Soon he wasn't selling printing on his travels; he was selling himself, in particular the Duncan Hines Seal of Approval. This sign became a guidepost for hungry travelers. If a restaurant had Hines's approval, that meant two things: It was good, and it was clean.

Soon Hines was so famous that Procter & Gamble asked him to lend his name to a cake mix. He tested the mix, approved, and signed on. It's been decades since the last edition of *Adventures in Good Eating,* and not many folks know Duncan Hines from restaurant reviews anymore. But the cake mix . . . we approve!

Two restaurants survive from Hines's first travel guide of 1934: the Beaumont Inn in Harrodsburg and the Country Inn at Historic Shaker Village of Pleasant Hill.

Each June Hines's hometown of Bowling Green celebrates his gustatory work with the Duncan Hines Festival—a weekend of good friends, good fun, and, oh yes, good food.

For festival information call (270) 792-4633 or visit www.duncan hinesfestival.com.

Return to Kentucky

Here's a scary thought: John Carpenter is from Kentucky.

Carpenter, who was raised in Bowling Green, wrote and directed the horror classic *Halloween*, as well as such other cult classics as *Escape from New York*, *They Live!*, and *Starman*.

Carpenter brought movie violence out of the closet and into the frame. His breakthrough film *Halloween* actually showed blood! Carpenter's tools of horror have long since been surpassed by bloodier, gorier fare. Watch *Halloween* today and you may be surprised how little gore there is. It's just that in 1978, most mainstream movie audiences thought of Hitchcock when they thought of horror, and Hitchcock seldom showed blood.

All this pioneering work from a guy who almost became a musician. You see, what brought Carpenter to Kentucky was music. His father moved the family from Carthage, New York, to Kentucky when he took a job heading the music department of Western Kentucky University. You can "hear" his musical influence in Carpenter's films—he wrote the score for sixteen of his nineteen films. Including, as you might expect, *Halloween*.

Ducktail Car
Bowling Green

If you don't now or never did sport a ducktail (or if you are female and you never hung on the arm of a ducktail-sporting male) in the 1950s, then you may want to skip this site. But if you understand the symbiotic relationship between men, their hair, and their cars, then you'll want to visit the National Corvette Museum, the only museum in the world devoted to that flashy sports car.

The museum is in Kentucky not because we had more ducktails per capita or Corvettes per capita, but because we are where it all started. Kentucky is where every Corvette has been made, and since they've all been manufactured in Bowling Green, it's only fitting that the city be the site of the museum.

There's a big anniversary celebration every year over Labor Day weekend, and Corvettes—and their owners—drive in from all over the country. You'll think you've gone back to the future.

While you're touring the museum, you can also check out the Corvette Hall of Fame. Sure, if you aren't a Corvette fanatic you might not recognize the names. But be aware: If you don't bow in front of the Harley Earl plaque, people may whisper. You see, Earl was the father of the Corvette. After watching Jaguars and MGs race at Watkins Glen, New York, he was convinced that America needed its own sports car. The tough part was convincing General Motors. But he managed to convince Ed Cole (another Hall of Famer) at GM's traditional "bow-tie" division, Chevrolet, and the rest is history.

The National Corvette Museum is at 350 Corvette Drive in Bowling Green. Call (270) 781-7973 or (800) 53-VETTE ('53 was, of course, the year of the first 'Vette), or visit www.corvettemuseum.com.

World's Largest Ham and Biscuit
Cadiz

This one will give you heartburn just from reading about it: a two-ton ham biscuit. That's not a misprint. That's 4,000 pounds of country ham and biscuit. And it's not a one-time thing. They've been baking this breakfast monstrosity every year since 1985 as part of Cadiz's Trigg County Country Ham Festival.

The Trigg pig gig every October swells this small town on the Tennessee border from 4,000 folks to 80,000 ham-lovers. That's a far cry from Farm-City Week, the event's predecessor, which was highlighted by a baking contest. In 1977 some Triggians put their heads together and realized the baking contest didn't really make sense since Trigg

County had long been known for its hams, not its baked goods. So they created the Country Ham Festival—and it's been growing every year.

They cook up a 720-pound biscuit in a custom-built 500,000 BTU oven, then lay on a little more than 3,000 pounds of cured pork. The biscuit was blessed by the *Guinness Book of World Records,* which had no previous record holder in that category (didn't have that category either).

The big biscuit isn't the only reason to attend Trigg's pig jig. There's a mess of small town fair–type events, including a pig derby, a greased pig-catching contest, and a kiss-a-pig competition. Don't worry if you get drafted into the latter event. Pigs don't kiss back.

For more information call the Cadiz-Trigg County Tourist Commission at (888) 446-6402 or visit www.hamfestival.com.

The World's First Media Event
Cave City

Floyd Collins was just born under a bad sign. Although he had great luck finding and exploring caves, he never profited from them.

At the height of the great "cave wars" of the 1920s, everyone but Collins seemed to prosper and receive vast wealth, even though he was the principal cave discoverer at the time. Many cave owners paid Collins to explore their caves, searching for new caverns, domes, and anything else that would attract more tourists. They hired Collins not only because he knew the caves in the Kentucky area better than anyone else, but because he was fearless—that, and he needed the money.

Collins owned a cave himself, Great Crystal Cave, but nearly went bankrupt. No one came to visit his cave because it was off the beaten track. Mammoth Cave was the area's biggest draw, and it left the smaller caverns clamoring for the public's attention. Some cave owners hired street performers to get the attention of travelers passing by. Some used more persuasive techniques, spreading rumors about "unfortunate" occurrences in other caves.

Cave owner George Morrison had a brilliant idea that set him apart from the rest. Morrison decided to build a new entrance to his cave that would link it to Mammoth Cave, opening the floodgates for tourists. He called it the "New Entrance to Mammoth Cave," and it worked. People began visiting Morrison's cave in droves.

Collins saw the potential in Morrison's idea, and on January 30, 1925, set out in Sand Cave with the intention of somehow linking his cave to Morrison's, thus being able to share the new entrance and finally getting the tourist dollars he had dreamed about. But as with everything else in his life, Collins would find himself out of luck. While in a crawl space so tight he couldn't put his hand between his chest and the wall, Collins kicked a rock, trapping his leg. News of Collins's predicament captivated the nation. Finally he had made news—front page news, no less, with more than sixteen newspapers sending reporters to cover the saga. The world read with anticipation, following all the details of how Collins was doing and the progress at freeing him. People wanted him to win!

Not only had Collins's luck turned with the media, but his financial luck also prospered. Tourists flooded his Great Crystal Cave in record numbers. Someone had to feed all the tourists and media, so Collins's family set up a hamburger restaurant near the entrance, where people could grab a bite to eat while waiting and watching. His family prospered further by selling souvenirs, everything from shirts to key chains to mugs—all commemorating Collins's ill fortune, physically anyway.

It all came to an end, though, after sixteen days. Rescue workers were unable to free Collins, and he died in the cave from exposure to the elements. Some of the townspeople who knew Collins said that dying was the best thing that ever happened to him. After years of missed success, fame, and fortune, he finally found it. He just didn't get to enjoy it.

The Floyd Collins Museum is inside the Wayfarer Bed and Breakfast, 1240 Old Mammoth Cave Road. For more information call (270) 773-3366 or visit the website www.cavecity.com/cave_city/floyd_collins.htm.

A Machine Gun By Any Other Name . . .

If it weren't for Kentuckian John Thompson, military men everywhere would be walking around carrying a Blish gun. And how intimidating would that be? But fortunately it was Thompson who worked out most of the weapon details on the submachine gun and thus lent it his name, the Tommy gun!

In 1914 Thompson retired from the army and began working full-time developing a lightweight personal gun that would fire bullets at a rapid pace. He was driven by two goals: one, to make lots of money; and two, to end the war in Europe. Thompson felt that if our boys had a small machine gun with rapid-fire ability, the war would be over. He worked hard at developing the gun, but he came across a stumbling block. For the gun to work properly, it needed a simple lock, called a breech lock.

While researching patent files he found a patent under the name of Navy Commander John Bell Blish, who had invented such a lock, known as the "Blish lock." In 1915 Thompson and Blish began work-ing together. Blish agreed to let Thompson use his lock in exchange for stock in an arms company Thompson planned to start. And he didn't insist that the Blish lock be used on the gun. In the spring of 1916 Thompson received financial backing from Thomas Fortune Ryan, a tobacco tycoon, and he began Auto Ordnance Corporation.

In 1918 Thompson's company invented the Annihilator I, a machine gun that lived up to its name: It could empty a twenty-round magazine in less than a second. Thompson thought he had struck gold, but as luck would have it the first shipment of Tommy guns destined for the war effort in Europe arrived at the docks of New York on November 11, 1918—the day the war ended. Thompson decided that because the war effort was a bust, he'd redesign the gun for personal use because, hey, everyone needs a machine gun. The first public demonstration of the personal submachine gun was in August 1920. By 1925 anyone with $225 could buy a Tommy gun at their local participating hardware store. And how many of them would have been sold if it had been called the Blish gun?

★ ★

Tacky Town USA
Cave City

Welcome to Cave City! Home of Mammoth Cave, Diamond Cavern, and cement statues.

While some may balk at the tackiness of Cave City, for the more adventurous tourist, Cave City is trash heaven! In addition to boasting

Quintessential Kentuckians

Happy Chandler, Happy Man

Born in Corydon, his name was Albert Benjamin, but nobody called him that. Even his wife called him Happy. It was a nickname he acquired during the 1920s as an ever-smiling student athlete at Transylvania College in Lexington.

Happy was a Harvard-educated lawyer, but you would never have known it. How many Harvard lawyers sing to their constituents? That's what Happy did when he first ran for Kentucky governor in 1935. He would later brag that he ran his campaign "with a seventy-five-dollar sound truck and a pitcher of ice water." During the campaign, he traveled to every county in the state, speaking five times each day, and closing each rally by singing college songs, hymns, and, of course, the state song, "My Old Kentucky Home."

He won, serving as governor from 1935 to 1939. Near the end of Happy's term the state's senior US senator, M. M. Logan, died. The opportunistic Happy, who always seemed to be more interested in his next job, resigned his post as governor, and his successor, Lt.

the world's largest cave system, Cave City also has more cement-statuary stores and miniature-golf parks than any other city in the country. The number is evenly divided, with either one or the other on every corner.

Everyone can be pleased with a stop at Cave City. Need a gift for that hard-to-shop-for person? Pick up a five-foot-tall cement statue of a rooster. Tired of being nagged by the kids with an endless banter of

Gov. Keen Johnson, succeeded him and appointed him to the senate job.

While in Washington, Happy became a fan of the Washington Senators baseball club, attending games when he should, perhaps, have been in the Senate chambers. He became friends with many baseball owners, and in 1945 he resigned his Senate seat to succeed Judge Kenesaw Mountain Landis as baseball's second commissioner.

It was during his tenure that Jackie Robinson broke baseball's color barrier, a historic event that Happy claimed to have championed. His detractors said he fought it until it happened and then grabbed the credit. He resigned in 1951, after the baseball team owners refused to extend his contract, and returned to Kentucky to run for governor again. He was elected and served from 1955 to 1959. A state law prevented him from succeeding himself. He ran again in '63, '67, and '71, but voters had tired of his act.

In his last years he became famous for singing "My Old Kentucky Home" at University of Kentucky home basketball games and for making outrageous comments at U.K. board of trustees meetings.

When Happy resigned as baseball commissioner in 1951, the publisher of the *Sporting News*, J. G. Taylor Spink, had this telling assessment of Happy: "Happy insisted on being himself." Happy Chandler was elected to baseball's Hall of Fame in 1982; he died in 1991.

"Are we there yet?" Stretch your legs out at Jellystone Park, Cave City's "amusement" park, complete with waterslides. Jellystone also makes a perfect photo op. You guessed it—they have a giant cement statue of Yogi Bear! If you prefer more adventurous amusement, stop at Guntown Mountain Amusement Park and see live gunfights (staged, of course) and saloon shows.

Still not convinced that Cave City is for you? Try one of their fine-dining restaurants. Joe's Diner is nestled in a metallic boxcar. The Sahara Steakhouse is right next to the Mammoth Cave Wildlife Museum, which features a display of animals found inside the caves and is also Kentucky's first and largest wildlife museum.

If those stops don't quite whet your appetite for Cave City, perhaps you'd be interested in the handful of antiques malls, craft stores, and "odd ball" gift shops the town has to offer. Where else will you find a fifteen-foot-tall knight? Yes, a knight in shining armor. He stands next to a fifteen-foot-high totem poll that can be yours as well.

Competition for the tourist dollar is fierce in Cave City. In fact, you'd be hard-pressed to find a store that didn't combine one or more of the more notable selling items in the city. You can buy gas and a cement statue of a gorilla at the truck stop. Mammoth Cave Wax Museum also sells rocks. And Diamond Caverns has branched out into antiques as well as guided tours. The list is endless. You'll just have to stop and immerse yourself in the culture of tack to fully appreciate it.

Cave City is located on Interstate 65, exit 55. For lots more information visit www.cavecity.com.

Wigwam Village
Near Cave City

Look! It's a wigwam! No, actually it's a tepee.

Frank Redford had a dream—a dream not of wealth, love, or world peace, but rather of a village built entirely of tepees where people could come together and experience a sense of community, Indian style. Actually, in the dream it was a village built of upside-down

More practical than a village of upside-down ice-cream cones.

ice-cream cones. Being the visionary he was—and knowing that a town made of food was nearly impossible—he decided to equate the geometric shape he was seeking with a tepee. It all worked out in the end.

In 1935 Redford built Wigwam Village in Horse Cave, Kentucky. You may be wondering, what exactly is a wigwam village? The village served more as a motel than actual tepee. The wigwams offered families a unique place to sleep, complete with the comforts of home, minus the phones and television. All the wigwams, built of steel and concrete, were set in a circular pattern opening to a "community center" where kids could play and parents could relax. Kind of like a tepee utopia.

★ ★

Wigwam Village was a success! So in 1937 Redford patented the idea and built five more villages—in Alabama, Florida, Louisiana, California, and Arizona. However, the popularity of the wigwam villages didn't last. There are only two left, the one in Cave City and one in Holbrook, Arizona.

Take Interstate 65, exit 53 (Cave City) to Highway 90 east, then north on Highway 31W (1.5 miles) or visit www.wigwamvillage.com.

Oh, Happy Day(s)
Corydon

Yes, there is a parade. No, Fonzie is not the grand marshal.

Every year Corydon comes alive on the Fourth of July to celebrate the Happy Days Festival. Corydon actually had no interest in creating a festival to compete with other counties and cities. The city really didn't have any need to celebrate anything at all. In the early 1990s Crawford Park, however, was donated to the city, although at the time of its donation it wasn't much of a park. Through volunteer efforts and fund-raising it became one. Not really knowing what to do with their park, the natives decided it would be a great place to have a festival and continue the fund-raising efforts and volunteer spirit.

Now that they had their very own festival they needed a name. There is no animal native to Corydon, nor is there a fruit, vegetable, or music style. Corydon's big claim to fame is that a former Kentucky governor was born there, but he wasn't just any governor. He was Albert Benjamin "Happy" Chandler, former baseball commissioner. Thus, the event was named the Happy Days Festival.

What will you find at the Happy Days Festival? World-famous ugly women. Corydon is known for its Womenless contest, where male notables of the city dress in drag to compete for the title of ugliest woman. You'll also find a parade of antique cars, mules, and wagons—and a heaping supply of barbecue.

For more information contact the Kentucky Department of Travel at (800) 225-8747.

Finger Pickin' Good

Drakesboro

There are all kinds of pickers out there, and while Kentucky has it's fair share of class-act nose pickers, it is (understandably) the thumb picker they choose to celebrate.

The National Thumb Picker's Hall of Fame is located in Muhlenberg County. Thumb picking is a unique style of guitar playing, where the fingers play the melody of the song and the thumb plays the bass. Done correctly, it resembles the sound of two guitars playing at one time.

This style of picking was initially made famous by Central City native and country music legend Merle Travis. Muhlenberg County is so proud of its picking son that every year they have a birthday bash on November 27. The tribute includes thumb picking contests and sixty gallons of beef stew served with corn bread and peach or apple cobbler, Merle's favorite meal.

For more information call the Central City/Muhlenberg County Chamber of Commerce at (270) 754-2360 or visit the website at www.ntphf.com.

The Dundee Masonic Lodge Goat

Dundee

The old saying about everybody talking about the weather doesn't apply in Dundee. In Dundee everybody talks about the weathervane.

The goat weathervane, that is. The Dundee Masonic Lodge is home to Dundee the Goat. Dundee has been atop the eighty-foot steeple of the building since 1902. It is the last surviving of three weathervanes brought from Dundee, Scotland, to the US in the 1890s. The other two were lost in fires—not winds!

The goat-shaped weathervane is made of zinc but only weighs ten pounds because it is hollow. The swaying of its butt determines the winds and storm probability. The town swears by its accuracy. The

Look up, in the sky! It's a goat!

goat has even been featured on the show *Ripley's Believe It or Not!* Every second weekend of August is Dundee Day and takes place in downtown Dundee near the lodge. It includes the smallest dog contest, baby contests, and lawn mower races. And the Dundee goat, showing its, uh, pointing prowess.

The Dundee Masonic Lodge is located at 11640 KY Highway 69 N. in Dundee. For more information check out the website at www.visit ohiocountyky.org.

I'd Like to Teach the World to . . .
Collect Coca-Cola Memorabilia
Elizabethtown

Newsflash: A Kentucky couple holds what is the world's largest privately owned collection of Coca-Cola memorabilia. There's really no competition other than the Coca-Cola Company itself in Atlanta, and that's not exactly "privately owned."

The Schmidts come by their Coke obsession naturally: The family has been an official Coca-Cola bottler since 1901. The collecting thing got started in the early 1970s with Jan and Bill Schmidt, who started collecting advertising memorabilia. It took off, and pretty soon the Schmidts had it all—from Coca-Cola serving trays to Coca-Cola calendars, drinking glasses, knives, playing cards, coolers, vending machines, ancient bottling equipment, toys, sheet music and, oh yes, Coca-Cola bottles, of which there are many styles.

You can't stroll through the museum without saying, "Oh, I remember that." The Schmidts like it when you say that; it means they've done their job.

The Schmidt Museum of Coca-Cola Memorabilia is a nonprofit corporation. You can contact the museum at (270) 234-1100 or visit www.schmidtmuseum.com.

★ ★

A Tale of Two Presidents

Fairview

The debate raged for many years: Is it the Civil War or the War Between the States? In Kentucky we have our own answer: It should be called the War Within the State. That's because in 1861 the president of the country, no matter your sympathies, was a Kentuckian. The president of the United States of America, Abe Lincoln, had been born near Hodgenville. And the president of the Confederate States of America, Jefferson Davis, had been born in Fairview, not far from Paducah.

The largest cast-concrete monument in the US marks the spot of Davis's birth in Fairview on June 3, 1808. He lived in the Bluegrass State only two years but he came back for school (St. Thomas of Aquinas Catholic School in Springfield) and college (Transylvania College in Lexington) before shipping out to attend the US Military Academy at West Point in New York in 1824. He even married a Kentucky girl, Sarah Knox Taylor, daughter of his commanding officer, General Zachary Taylor, but she died three months later of malaria.

Davis had a distinguished career—Mexican War hero, congressman and senator from Mississippi, secretary of war under Franklin Pierce—until he cast his lot with the losing side in the Civil War.

At a Confederate reunion in 1907, one of his generals, Simon Bolivar Buckner, suggested a monument to honor Davis. The result is a 351-foot-tall obelisk resting on a foundation of Kentucky limestone. The monument looks startlingly similar to the Washington Monument, but don't mention that. Folks around here don't want to hear it.

The Davis Monument is one of seventy-two Confederate monuments in the state, compared to only two Union ones—this despite the fact that Kentucky sent three times as many troops to the Union as to the Confederacy and was officially neutral during the Civil War. Or is that the War Between the States?

The Jefferson Davis Monument State Historic Site is nine miles east of Hopkinsville on US Highway 68. For more information call (270) 886-1765 or visit http://parks.ky.gov/parks/historicsites/jefferson-davis/default.aspx.

★ ★

Where Jimi Hendrix Broke His Ankle

Fort Knox

It's probably more famous as the place where all the gold is. But some of us prefer to think of it as the place where Jimi Hendrix broke his ankle while in basic training. It's Fort Knox, home of the Bullion Depository.

As surprising as it may seem, a "bullion depository" is not where they store soup broth. The Bullion Depository in Fort Knox is actually where our nation houses the largest amount of US gold reserves. The depository was completed in December 1936 and was in use by January 1937 by the US Mint. More than 750 tons of reinforced steel surrounded by 670 tons of structural steel help keep the gold bars safe—not to mention the vault doors that weigh more than twenty tons each. In addition to being one of the safest places on earth, the depository is equipped with its own emergency power plant, water system, and shooting range in the basement—so that the guards can keep in top form. No one is allowed down in the depository itself, but you can view it from a second-level overlook area. Each gold bar inside is worth approximately $16,000. No single person has the combination to the safe. Instead, several people have a combination and for the doors to open, each one must put his or her code in.

Fort Knox isn't only home to the nation's largest warehouse of gold; it also houses our nation's largest US Army museum. On January 16, 1932, the First Cavalry Regiment, the army's oldest mounted unit, relocated to Fort Knox and left its horses behind. The Armored Forces began in July 1940. The General George Smith Patton Jr. Museum opened in 1949, proudly displaying the nation's progression of weaponry through the ages. Today Fort Knox has the largest collection of tanks, guns, and army machinery in the free world—also gold.

Call (502) 624-3812 for information. No visitors are allowed at the Bullion Depository, but you can visit the Patton Museum at 554 Fayette Avenue (near the Chaffee Avenue entrance to Fort Knox). Take Chaffee Avenue east off Dixie Highway (US Highway 31). Turn left on Ballard, then left on Fayette. Call the museum at (502) 943-8977 or visit its website at www.generalpatton.org.

Kentucky's First UFO
Fort Knox

The UFO sighting craze that began in Roswell, New Mexico, in 1947 arrived in Kentucky shortly after New Year's Day 1948. Tower control at Godman Air Force Base in Fort Knox picked up an unidentified flying object on its radar on January 7, 1948, and sent Captain Charles Mantrell scrambling in his P-51 jet. As Mantrell approached the UFO, he radioed back: "It appears to be a metallic object . . . tremendous in size . . . directly ahead and slightly above. . . . I am trying to close for a better look."

That was the last transmission received from Mantrell. He crashed his plane and died, and no one knows to this day if what he saw was a genuine UFO or another of those ubiquitous weather balloons.

Fort Knox is located on US Highway 31 West just south of Louisville, but don't try to get too close. That's where all the gold is, too, so they aren't exactly receptive to tourists. But you can look up in the skies south of the base and imagine what it must have been like that cold January day in 1948 when the first UFO invaded Kentucky.

The Tobacco State—Birthplace of the Nicotine Patch
Franklin

There's no irony here, not much. Kentucky, land of tobacco, is also home to the man who invented a product to help smokers kick their cigarette habit.

Franklin native Dr. Frank Etscorn graduated from Western Kentucky University in 1973 with a master's degree in experimental psychology. Etscorn developed the nicotine patch as a fluke: He accidentally spilled liquid nicotine on his arm while working on a research project at New Mexico Tech. A non-smoker, Etscorn's eyes lit up. Just that brief skin contact gave him the sensation of having smoked a pack of cigarettes. That's when the idea hit him of inventing a patch that could feed nicotine through the skin, helping addicts kick the habit. Etscorn toiled on the product, perfected it, and sold it to a pharmaceutical company, making a fortune in the process. In 1992 both *Time* and *Fortune* magazines named the nicotine patch one of the best new products of the year.

Etscorn has been working on a number of important research projects, including a method to thwart termites by treating lumber with hot chili peppers.

Penn's Store's Great Outhouse Blowout and Race
Gravel Switch

This is exactly what it sounds like. People mount outhouses (an outhouse is an outdoor bathroom, for the uninitiated) on wheels and race them down the road. The winner gets, uh, the honor of being known as the winner. The event, which lasts four days, is held every October.

But it's worth visiting Penn's Store even if you visit out of outhouse season. That's because the store is the oldest in the country in continuous operation by the same family. Gabriel Jackson Penn bought the place in 1850 (it had been in business since at least 1845), renamed it Penn's Store, and it's been in the Penn family ever since.

The outhouse race is a recent addition. The Penn people started it in 1992 when the store got its first outhouse. That's right, the place had been operating for 142 years without a bathroom. But there are a lot of nice, big trees nearby.

There's more to the Great Outhouse Blowout than outhouse racing; there's also fiddling, whittling, a gathering of herb enthusiasts, and the much-anticipated Parade of Privies.

Penn's Store is at 257 Penn's Store Road in Gravel Switch. You can reach them at (859) 332-7715 or (859) 332-7706.

The Penn people caution that their place is not easy to find. Here are their directions from the Renfro Valley exit on Interstate 75. "Turn left onto Highway 461 and follow until it intersects with Highway 150. Turn west (right) onto Highway 150. At Stanford, turn left onto

Highway 27. Then turn right onto Highway 150 again and go through downtown Stanford. Turn west (left) onto Highway 78. Turn north (right) onto Highway 243. Follow for approximately six miles. Just before Highway 243 intersects with Highway 37, turn left onto a side road. Penn's Store is straight ahead." It's next to a popular swimming hole, where the Little South Creek meets North Rolling Fork.

For more information visit the website at www.pennsstore.com/events/blowout.htm.

A Mooving Experience
Greensburg

Technically it's the Greensburg Rotary Club—Double Cola/Ski Cow Days Festival. But everybody around Greensburg just calls it Cow Days.

It really isn't that exciting—unless you are a cow. Just the usual small town festival stuff: food vendors, arts and crafts competitions, an antique tractor show, a frog-croaking contest (but not a cow-mooing contest), a pipe-smoking contest, a cow giveaway, and a flea market. And they take their flea market seriously. The vendor contract specifies: "We will not allow anyone to sell Snap-Pops, Smelly Gas, Hair Color Spray, or any other object considered offensive by the Greensburg Rotary Club." Kind of makes you want to buy a can of Smelly Gas, doesn't it?

But you have to admit, Cow Days is a great name for a festival.

Cow Days is held every September. For more information call (270) 932-4298.

Robert Penn Warren Birthplace Museum
Guthrie

Anyone who says Kentucky lacks class—and, hey, there are a couple—has obviously never heard of Robert Penn Warren. Warren was appointed as the nation's first official poet laureate in 1986. By that time he had already earned three Pulitzer Prizes for works in poetry and fiction, and is the only writer to have done so. His best known work is the novel *All the King's Men*. The novel is loosely based on the life of Louisiana Governor Huey Long. Spoiler alert, both Long and the character based on Long were shot at the height of their political careers. Warren also never denied that his character was based on Long, but in true intellectualist fashion said that who it was based on or the political career of that person did not matter. He concluded that it was merely a means to show deeper issues. The novel was adapted in 1949 and 2006 for the big screen. The 1949 version was critically acclaimed, winning three Oscars, but was said to deviate significantly from the novel. The 2006 version, however, received dismal reviews, even with an all-star cast, but was much more in line with the original novel. Warren's childhood small, red brick house in Guthrie is open to the public. It contains items from Warren's life and works.

The Robert Penn Warren Birthplace Museum is located at Third and Cherry Streets in Guthrie. For more information check out the website at www.robertpennwarren.com/birthpla.htm.

Lawyer Lincoln's First Case . . . Defending Himself!
Hawesville

The Lincolns were living on Pigeon Creek in Indiana in 1827 when eighteen-year-old Abe took a job at nearby Posey's Landing, running a ferryboat across the Anderson River, which empties into the Ohio. Looking to make a little money on the side, Abe built a rowboat and took to ferrying passengers out to the paddle wheelers that steamed up and down the Ohio.

The Dill brothers, who operated a ferry across the Ohio in Kentucky, thought Abe was stealing some of their business. They had an exclusive license to operate a ferryboat across the river at that spot, and they convinced the local constable, Squire Samuel Pate, to haul young Abe up on charges of operating an illegal ferryboat.

The *Commonwealth of Kentucky vs. Abraham Lincoln* was tried in Pate's home at Little Yellow Banks across the river from Troy, Indiana, near the future site of Hawesville in the spring of 1827. After

★ ★

hearing the charge, Lincoln argued that his boat did not cross the river. And if it didn't cross the river, it couldn't be a ferry, so he didn't need a license. Squire Pate was impressed with Lincoln's presentation and logic and dismissed the case. But he also advised Lincoln that he should familiarize himself with the law before he got into any new businesses.

Lincoln took the constable's words at face value. He began reading his friend David Turnham's *Revised Laws of Indiana* and made frequent forays back across the Ohio to observe the proceedings in Pate's court. Seven years later, after election to the Illinois legislature, he took up formal study of the law; in 1836 he was licensed to practice in Illinois.

Pate House is located three miles west of Hawesville on Highway 334. Lincoln's case was tried in the east room of the log house. For more information visit the website at www.hancockky.us/History/historichomes.htm.

"M" is for the Money That We Spend on Mother's Day Each Year
Henderson

Mary Wilson was a teacher at the Henderson School in 1887 when she got the idea to have her students honor their mothers. They put together a musical program, called it their Mother's Day Musical, and invited all their moms to the schoolhouse to watch. It quickly became an annual event, and Mrs. Wilson traveled to other local schools to help them with their musical celebrations.

She didn't live to see her little celebration declared a national holiday in 1916. In one of the ironies of life, Mary Wilson was never a mother. She died giving birth.

It should be noted that West Virginia disputes this story, claiming Mother's Day as the invention of Anna Maria Reeves Jarvis of Grafton, West Virginia, who founded the Mother's Day Work Clubs, which provided domestic help for mothers with tuberculosis. Jarvis organized many mothers' celebrations in her life and lobbied President Woodrow

Wilson to make Mother's Day a holiday. She convinced her minister to conduct a Mother's Day service on May 12, 1907, and this is recognized everywhere else as the first Mother's Day celebration in the United States.

In Kentucky, we know better. Mary Wilson invented Mother's Day two decades earlier.

The Henderson School was at the corner of Green and Center Streets. Mary Wilson lived for many years at 232 South Main Street in what is now known as the Towles-Sasseen House.

Lincoln's Boyhood Home . . . Sort Of . . . Maybe
Hodgenville

Kentucky's license plates should say *Land of Lincoln.* After all, he was born here, his people were from here, and his best friends lived here. Instead, Kentucky's license plates read *Bluegrass State.* Illinois gets to call itself the "Land of Lincoln."

It could have been different—except that Kentucky and Lincoln have had a troubled history, going back to his first legal case: defending himself against Kentucky, which was charging him with operating a ferry illegally.

They later tore down the cabin he was born in. That was in 1870, and the place had been nothing more than a corncrib for years. You see, in 1870 Lincoln was not yet a Kentucky legend. There was that Union thing. And while Kentucky was divided about secession and the Civil War, it was not divided about Lincoln. Didn't like him. Not one bit. Gave him a mere 1 percent of the state's vote in the 1860 presidential election. So when the family that owned the Knob Creek farm where the Lincolns had once lived tore down the cabin in 1870, there wasn't one word of protest.

His birthplace—a tiny one-room log cabin ten miles to the west—we tore that down long before he even made it to Washington. Who knew? So what you will see on the site of his birth and the site of his boyhood home are "symbolic" cabins.

★ ★

Let's begin at the beginning. Abraham Lincoln was born in a log cabin on Sinking Creek Farm on February 12, 1809. Go to the birth site today and you can see that cabin, or at least what has been billed, off and on, for a century as the log cabin of his birth. There's absolutely no proof that it is. In fact the Park Service hands out a brochure that notes, "Although its early history is obscure, extensive research suggests that the cabin displayed in the Memorial Building is not the birthplace of Abraham Lincoln." What it is is a cabin that was constructed in 1861 from a decaying log house that sat on the old Lincoln farm site. There may even be a few logs from the original. No one really knows.

In 1894 a New York restaurateur bought the 1861 cabin and sent it on tour around the country, exhibiting it in Buffalo, Nashville, and even New York's Central Park. The thing was disassembled and put in storage on Long Island, then rescued in 1900 by Mark Twain and a group of celebrities, who raised the money to buy the logs and ship them back to Kentucky.

In 1911 the eighteen-by-sixteen-foot cabin was reconstructed inside a new marble-and-granite memorial reached only by climbing up fifty-six steps—one step for each year Lincoln lived. Let's just call it Lincoln's Symbolic Birthplace. Of course Lincoln lived there only two years before his dad lost title to the farm. The family moved ten miles east to what Lincoln called the "Knob Creek place," another log cabin.

And sure enough, drive over and you can see yet another Lincoln log cabin. This one was reconstructed in 1931 on the original Knob Creek site, using logs that no one has ever claimed came from the original cabin. No, here they claim some of the logs came from the Austin Gollaher cabin. There is a connection: Gollaher once saved young Abe from drowning in Knob Creek. Let's call it Lincoln's Symbolic Boyhood Home.

The Lincolns left Knob Creek in 1816, crossing the Ohio River to Indiana at Cloverport. A historical market denotes the spot.

You can go a little further back in time, Lincoln time, with a visit to nearby Lincoln Homestead State Park. Here, within shouting range of a golf course, is where the first Abraham Lincoln, the future president's grandfather, was killed by Indians. A replica of the family's cabin sits on the site, where tradition has it young Thomas Lincoln, Abe's father, grew up. That would be the Symoblic Ancestral Home. Also nearby, relocated from its original site a mile away, is a two-story log cabin, the Francis Berry house, where Nancy Hanks was living when she met Thomas Lincoln. It's not symbolic; it's the real deal.

Abraham Lincoln Birthplace National Historic Site is located three miles south of Hodgenville on US Highway 31 East. For information call (270) 358-3137. Lincoln's boyhood home, Knob Creek Farm, is located seven miles northeast of Hodgenville on US Highway 31 East. For information call (502) 549-3741. Lincoln Homestead State Park is located five miles north of Springfield on Highway 438. For information call (859) 336-7461 or visit the website www.nps.gov/abli/index.htm.

Lincoln Days

Every October, Hodgenville celebrates its Lincoln heritage with Lincoln Days, a festival that includes a rail-splitting competition, a crafts festival, and a parade of Lincoln impersonators. You haven't seen anything until you've seen two dozen Lincoln look-alikes (or sort of look-alikes) walking down a city street.

For information call (270) 358-8710.

★ ★

Edgar Cayce, "The Sleeping Prophet"

Hopkinsville

You are getting sleepy, very sleepy. When you awake you will be able
to place yourself in a trance and predict world events. Does this seem
hard to believe? For Edgar Cayce, hypnosis was just the beginning.

Born in Hopkinsville, the "sleeping prophet" began his life as a
deeply religious farm boy. As a child, Cayce recalled being able to see
ghosts, who would talk to him and help him out. One of the more
prominent spirits he claimed to see was that of a gray-haired woman
who would come to him when he needed her the most—while studying for school. According to Cayce, the apparition instructed him to lie
down, and when he awoke he knew all he needed to know to pass his
exams. Apparently she wasn't much better at school than Cayce. He
ended up dropping out after the eighth grade.

When Cayce was twenty-one years old, he developed a strange
condition that paralyzed his vocal cords. Not being able to talk hurt
his career as a salesman. Cayce needed help, and he needed it fast.
Doctors prescribed remedies that didn't work, so Cayce turned to
hypnotist Al Layne. Layne taught Cayce how to place himself under a
"healing self-induced trance."

The trance worked. In fact, according to Cayce, it worked too well.
While under a trance, Cayce was able to predict the future. He could
also diagnose patients' illnesses with just a name and address. On
October 9, 1910, the *New York Times* published an article on Cayce's
talents, "Illiterate Man Becomes a Doctor When Hypnotized; Strange
Power Shown By Edgar Cayce Puzzles Physicians." The article brought
Cayce national fame.

Soon Cayce was bombarded with requests for health readings and
"life" readings, where he could tell someone who they were in a past
life. Cayce also began making grim predictions of the future, all of
which were recorded and published. Some of the more notable predictions were the rise of Atlantis in 1968 and the second coming of Christ
in 1998, which would be immortalized with a shift in the Earth's poles

and "superquakes." Cayce also saw himself reborn in post-apocalypse Nebraska in 2100.

In 1931 Cayce moved to Virginia Beach and formed the Association for Research and Enlightenment (ARE). On New Year's Day 1945, Cayce became ill and predicted to everyone, from a trance of course, that he would be miraculously cured of his illness. Three days later, Cayce died at the age of sixty-seven.

There's a Cayce display at the Pennyroyal Area Museum, 217 East Ninth Street; (270) 887-4270.

The Woody Winfree Fire Transportation Museum
Hopkinsville

The Hopkinsville downtown firehouse was completed in 1905 with an eighty-five-foot clock tower. It burned to the ground two decades later. A little irony there.

But that's not the end of the story; it's only the beginning. The firehouse was rebuilt to its previous glory and after it outlived its use as a firehouse it was turned into a museum by the city of Hopkinsville. Only problem, the town didn't have any artifacts for the museum. Enter Woody Winfree. Woody was a local volunteer firefighter, a State Farm insurance agent, and, happily, a collector of fire memorabilia. The museum includes his collection of old fire trucks, including the city's first truck, buggies, wagons, a sleigh, and a large collection of Christian County license plates.

The most amazing exhibit is a record book detailing one hundred years worth of calls placed to the fire department. The first entry was placed to the Pearless Fire Company, a progenitor of the Hopkinsville Fire Company, in 1892. In those days, fires were fought by horse-drawn "fire wagons." Steam-driven fire pumps were just introduced, so even if the station could afford the new technology, the large pumps still had to be dragged by the horses from the station to the fire.

The Woody Winfree Fire Transportation is located at 217 E. Ninth Street in Hopkinsville. For more information check out the website at www.visithopkinsville.com/events/DisplayAttraction.asp?ID=46.

Little Green Men— or Pink Elephants?

Some say it never happened. Some say it happened but not the way you heard it. Danny McCord isn't sure. "My aunt was a religious woman, and she swore to her dying day that it was aliens," he says.

Something happened on that October night in 1955, and it deeply affected the people of Kelly, a wide place in the road eight miles north of Hopkinsville. They say that Gaither McGehee, his wife and sons, and a neighbor boy were sitting at the kitchen table that night when they saw a light in the field. Being Kentuckians, they went for their guns and went for the light. They would later claim that they saw little green men emerge from a UFO in the field. The Kentuckians and the aliens exchanged gunfire before the Kentucky boys retreated inside the house. When the sheriff investigated the next day, he found a wooden house pockmarked with square bullet holes. He vowed to newspaper reporters that it had to have been aliens. "These are not drinking people," he pointed out.

When I investigated recently, the fellow who ran the bait shop nearby told me the sheriff didn't know those people. "They were carnival people." He swore it was just a drunken brawl. How to explain the square bullet holes? "That's from the bullets coming out of the house, not going in." Sad to report, the house was torn down in the seventies.

Aliens or alcohol? You decide.

Stink Cave

Horse Cave

Pop quiz: Horse Cave was named "Horse Cave" because: (a) a horse-powered pumping device was used to remove water from the cave; (b) a horse fell over the cliff leading into the cave and died; (c) a gang of thieves used the cave to hide the horses they stole from local towns-people; (d) it's not called Horse Cave; it's actually called "Stink Cave"; or (e) all of the above.

The correct answer: (e) all of the above.

Nestled at the bottom of a sinkhole, Horse Cave has a freshwater river going through the middle of it. Shortly after it was first discovered, locals used the resource for their water supply, using horses to cart numerous pumping devices and pipes to lift the water from the cave to the surface. The cave became a tourist attraction in 1925 when Dr. Harry B. Thomas opened it for tours and social gatherings. At the attraction's peak, groups of socialites would make the trek down steep stairs, over the water, and through the mud to the cave's largest dome, where they held dances during the warm summer months.

Prosperous times were short-lived for Horse Cave, and in 1943 it was closed. For years locals had not only been using the cave's water resources but also polluting it. Area townspeople built their outhouses near sinkholes that led directly to the river flowing inside the cave. The sinkholes, a natural phenomenon in this region, also became the town dump, filled with trash, dead animals, and anything that wouldn't burn. The pollution was so bad that a geologist touring the cave stated that the river was pitch black with feces and waste. As you can imagine, the pollution had a profound effect on the town; a horrendous stench filled the air and was only compounded by the summer heat. Thomas was forced to close the cave—not for a lack of interested people willing to put up with the stench to see it, but because the smell was so bad people passed out before they could get to the entrance.

In 1970 the government got involved and issued a decree that the townspeople could no longer dump their trash or waste in any area that would affect the cave. It took a while, but in 1983, after being closed for forty years, Horse Cave reopened for business.

While the townspeople still refer to the cave as Horse Cave and the cave does sit in Horse Cave City, if you go there, you won't find it. As part of the restoration efforts and efforts to get the townspeople behind the idea of cleaning up the pollution, a contest was held to rename the cave. It is now called Hidden River Cave. However, it still goes by Horse Cave, and Stink Cave, and . . . well, you get the idea.

The cave was cleaned up and reopened in 1993. There are guided tours daily from Memorial Day to Labor Day. The rate for an adult is $10; children can tour for less. The Hidden River Cave is located in the American Cave Museum at 119 East Main Street, in Horse Cave.

For more information check out the website at www.horsecave ky.com.

The World's Largest Apple Pie

Liberty

There's nothing more American than apple pie and Big Wheels! For the last full week of September, Casey County kicks off the fall season with the Casey County Apple Festival, held in downtown Liberty. More than 50,000 people attend the event every year, making it one of the largest festivals in the state. A fall festival is common for Kentucky. In fact, most counties have one, and some even have an apple festival. But they don't have what Casey County has . . . a 3,500-pound apple pie.

The Casey County Apple Festival is home to the world's largest apple pie. The pie takes three hours to build and ten hours to cook, is ten feet in diameter and eight inches deep, and serves 8,500. While most people come to the festival for the pie, there are other things that keep them coming back year after year, including crafts, vendor booths, and a Big Wheels race. Where else can you eat a piece of the world's largest apple pie and see grown men compete on Big Wheels?

For information on the festival, call (606) 787-6241 or visit www .caseycountyapplefestival.org.

Moonshine Capital of the World

Because there's no official government designation for Moonshine Capital of the World, there are a number of claimants to the title: Climax, Virginia, stages an annual Moonshiners Jamboree. Cosby, Tennessee, in the foothills of the Great Smoky Mountains, also lays claim to the title, as does Rocky Mount, Virginia, which managed to get the *New York Times* to call it "the moonshine capital of the world." Brasstown, North Carolina, used to claim the title. It now prefers to be called the Opossum Capital of the World.

But if you've ever seen the lay of the land in Land Between the Lakes, you know this is the place. It doesn't get any more remote than this.

In *The Antecedents of Southern Organized Crime*, Dr. Gary W. Potter of Eastern Kentucky University calls the area a "very important moonshine enclave." He notes that the Golden Pond area between the Cumberland and Tennessee Rivers produced a moonshine whiskey that was highly sought during Prohibition. "In an area with no more than 300 inhabitants, and no airport, it is said that dozens of planes flew in and out on a weekly basis carrying the prized brew to Chicago and New York." The Capone syndicate, Meyer Lansky, Bugsy Siegel, and Owney "the Killer" Madden, all looked to Golden Pond for their hooch. Potter says, "Moonshining was so organized and demand so intense that each hollow had as many as fifteen stills operating."

Of course that was a long time ago. But once the Moonshine Capital of the World, always the Moonshine Capital of the World.

★ ★

Pulling a Fast One
Mammoth Cave

"Are you afraid of snakes? That's okay, because there are no snakes at Mike's Mystery House."

Cheesy opening, yes, but this is how the tour of Mike's Mystery House begins. Located just outside of Mammoth Cave National Park, Mike's Mystery House is, in fact, no real mystery. For a dollar, visitors can take a tour of a "gravity-defying" area, conveniently located behind Big Mike's Rock and Gift Shop.

Admission to the tour includes one-liner jokes, endless puns and double entendres, and a maze of black lighting that helps add to the spooky kitsch of it all. In addition to being one of the rare places on earth that has gravity-pull centers, Mike's Mystery House is also one

The entrepreneurial spirit is alive and well at Mike's Mystery House.

Say hello to Big Mo at Mammoth Cave.

of the world's largest tributes to Spencer's Gifts stores, a fact that is brought up numerous times during the journey, as you are encouraged to touch the glow-in-the-dark posters, electric balls, and lava lamps.

Guests get to feel firsthand the effect of the gravitational pull in the house. You can crawl up a wall, sit in a chair that is placed against the wall midway up, and walk up the wall using some strategically placed steps. As you wind yourself down from the excitement of the "mystery spot," with the aid of some fun-house mirrors, the tour comes to an end. But that's not all! Luckily for you, the tour just happens to end right inside Mike's store, where you can stock up on various souvenirs, cups, shirts, and rocks. There's no admission charge to tour the souvenir shop. But that doesn't mean it won't cost you.

You'll feel the pull at 566 Old Mammoth Cave Road in Cave City. For more information call (270) 773-5144 or visit the website at www .mammothcave.com.

★ ★

Muffler Men
Monticello and Somerset

They're everywhere! They're everywhere!

They are giant fiberglass men stalking the landscape—some holding axes, others carrying hamburgers or tires.

They're known among roadside Americana aficionados as Muffler Men, because many of them were originally purchased by muffler shops.

The Muffler Men generally stand twenty to twenty-five feet tall, with square jaws and arms poised for carrying. They were manufactured in the 1960s and '70s by the California firm International Fiberglass and were installed on storefront rooftops all across America. One defining characteristic of a Muffler Man is that he has been moved from his original location and remodeled to promote a different kind of business. Thus, Paul Bunyan may have put down his axe and taken up holding a gas pump. The other defining characteristic is that the Muffler Man's right palm faces up and his left palm faces down. Anything else is a counterfeit.

There are two Muffler Men in southeastern Kentucky. The one in Somerset, a Paul Bunyan Muffler Man, is in "The Mountains" region at 601 US Highway 27, three miles north of town, next to a Super 8 Motel.

The one in Monticello is also a Paul Bunyan look-alike. He now resides on private property. It's on Highway 1546, about three miles west of Highway 90 West, next to Rector's Flat Baptist Church.

Kentucky Stonehenge
Munfordville

Have you ever wanted to visit England's Stonehenge, but can't seem to come up with the cash? Not a problem. A complete replica of the mysterious prehistoric site stands in Munfordville. It was created by a Munfordville resident and rock hound Chester Fryer. Fryer used rocks from miles around to create the structure on the grounds of his residence. It's not an authentic replica—it's no Clonehenge—because Fryer followed his own design. He wanted to improve on the original.

Kentucky's Clonehenge.

★ ★

Fryer had extra rocks so he also created a replica Garden of Gethsemane and another display that he just calls Twisted Rock, which is what it is.

To get to Kentucky Stonehenge take exit 65 from Interstate 65 onto US Highway 31 West. Turn right onto Lynn Avenue and go up the hill. You'll know it when you get there.

World's Strangest Baaaabecue Sandwich
Owensboro

Ask for a barbecue sandwich at any of Owensboro's half-dozen or so barbecue eateries, and you may be surprised. Barbecue in Owensboro isn't pork, as it is in most of America. And it isn't beef, as it is in Texas. It's mutton. Mutton! Sheep meat! And no one in town can tell you for sure why that is.

Henry Etta Schauberger and Stan LeMaster, who wrote the definitive history of Owensboro barbecue for the Daviess County Historical Society in 1970, could only conjecture that it was because the area was a major sheep-producing region during the Civil War. But they also note that after the turn of the twentieth century, sheep were getting scarce because of rampaging bands of dogs. Whatever the reason, accept it. And accept mutton. It is, as Andy Griffith used to say, goooooooood—a bit stronger than beef, not as sweet as pork, but tasty—and different.

Owensboro has declared itself the "Barbecue Capital of the World." Just insert "Mutton" before "Barbecue" and you won't get any argument anywhere. Every May they celebrate the fact with the International Bar-B-Q Festival, an event that draws more than 100,000 people to Owensboro's riverfront (it's the Ohio) to watch church cooking teams compete for bragging rights. Tourists benefit as well: Once the judging has concluded, the churches sell that barbecue to anybody with a five-dollar bill and a big appetite.

For more information on the International Bar-B-Q Festival, call (270) 926-6938 or visit www.bbqfest.com.

"What's for lunch?" . . . "Mutton, honey."
COURTESY OF KENTUCKYTOURISM.COM

Washington County Sorghum and Tobacco Festival
Springfield

It's not an appetizing sounding combination. Not many people would naturally put sorghum and tobacco together, but when both grow in abundance in your town, what else are you going to do? Every year Springfield hosts the Washington County Sorghum Festival.

To fully appreciate the festival, you first need to know what sorghum is. Sorghum is a grass-like plant that is ground and the juices extracted to make a molasses-like product.

★ ★

Held the first week of October, the festival draws a crowd of about 15,000 and even has its own motto: "Always a major success for the whole family." And it is. There is a buffet breakfast every morning so that visitors can sample the rich molasses grown in the fields out back and made next door. After breakfast, you can light up a cigarette and

Jesse James Robs Bank; Everyone Happy

Jesse James robbed the Southern Bank in Russellville, and they're still proud of the fact today. But James's connection to Kentucky began long before his days of crime. His parents, Robert and Zerelda James, were married in Stamping Ground, Kentucky, and his brother, Frank, was born there. Just before Jesse was born, the family moved to Missouri; shortly thereafter, his father deserted the family and moved west, caught up in the gold rush. He never did find his riches, though. He didn't really have much time to do so. After arriving on the West Coast, Robert James died of food poisoning. Some people speculate that the absence of his father is what led Jesse to a life of crime. Others say that he really didn't commit the crimes attributed to him. Regardless, his legend grew, and the Southern Deposit Bank was just a stopping point for him.

Jesse ran with a gang of bandits, which included his older brother and random criminals who wanted in on easy hits. Jesse was the youngest and least experienced of the group—and some say not the brightest in the pack, either. He was the prettiest, however, and he knew it. Jesse loved to have his picture taken and did so at nearly every stop he and the gang made. It was his good looks that

watch molasses being made. As we all know, there's nothing slower than molasses! Maybe you should bring a carton of cigarettes—it's going to be a long festival.

For festival information call (859) 336-3810, ext. 1.

distinguished him from the rest of the group; thus newspapers and people attributed many of the crimes to him alone.

On March 20, 1868, Jesse and his crew entered the Southern Deposit Bank at Sixth and Main Streets in Russellville. Reports at the time said that they walked away with $12,000 to $14,000. Later reports claimed, however, that Jesse and his brother were not even there. The initial crime report states that five men were involved in the heist. Eyewitnesses were able to describe each man in detail. While the men described did match the descriptions of some of the men known to have run with Jesse and his brother, no one said that the James boys were there. After the reports had been taken, a Detective Blyh came down from Louisville, investigated, and decided that Jesse had not only been there but was in charge of the entire operation.

With the announcement that Jesse James and his gang had robbed their bank, Russellville became a media boomtown, and Jesse would be linked to Kentucky once again. After a fifteen-year crime spree that included an April 1872 bank robbery in Columbia, Kentucky, Jesse James announced his retirement—well, not publicly, but to the boys in his gang. In December 1881 he adopted the alias Tom Howard and rented a home in St. Joseph, Missouri. But retirement only made Jesse a target. Four months later, a man named Bob Ford broke into "Mr. Howard's" home and shot him in the head.

★ ★

The Town Nobody Wants
Static

The town of Static, on the Kentucky-Tennessee border near Dale Hollow Lake, is an orphan, rejected by both states. Kentucky says it's in Tennessee, and Tennessee says it's in Kentucky. Visit and you may decide they're both right. It's nowhere. It definitely lives up to its name; there's not a lot happening.

Quintessential Kentuckians

The High Lonesome Sound of Bill Monroe

Elvis may have been the King of Rock and Roll, but he wasn't its father. Neither was Louis Armstrong the father of jazz. But as sure as can be, Bill Monroe was the father of bluegrass. Monroe, born in tiny Rosine, in 1911, invented the musical form, gave it its name, and was its embodiment until his death in 1996.

Monroe started out in a conventional country band with his brothers, Charlie and Birch. In the early 1930s the three worked at an East Chicago oil refinery during the week and played house parties on the weekends. They even danced (yes, danced!) on the WLS radio "Barn Dance" some weekends. Such was the financial structure of country music at the time that its finest musicians had to square dance and hold day jobs to pay the bills. Country music was essentially a regional music, and record sales were not in the Kenny Chesney range.

Birch left the band in 1934 when the boys landed a sponsor, a laxative company, that wanted them to move to Iowa. Bill and Charlie continued performing, eventually recording for Bluebird Records.

The major industries in town are selling gasoline and selling lottery tickets. You'll recognize the Kentucky side of town immediately. That's where all the lottery ticket signs are. Before you leave, you should check out an interesting highway sign on Tennessee Highway 111. It directs the traveler to nearby Jamestown—and it points both ways.

To reach Static, go right on US Highway 127 southbound to Jamestown, Tennessee. Go left on US Highway 127 to Jamestown, Kentucky. Then go figure.

But despite their brotherly love, the two didn't get along. Charlie, eight years older, gregarious and domineering, was the lead singer and the group leader. Bill, who was born with crossed eyes and poor vision, was a loner with a bit of a chip on his shoulder. They couldn't even agree on the direction their music should take, so they split in 1938. Charlie kept the recording contract; Bill got his musical independence.

He formed an all-string band, where the emphasis was on the instruments. The vocals, usually performed by Monroe, were tight with what he called a "high lonesome sound." He first called the gang Bill Monroe and the Kentuckians, later changing the name to Bill Monroe and the Blue Grass Boys. They played church-style harmonies to a dance beat with hints of blues and jazz. Their big break came when they played an upbeat version of Jimmie Rodgers's "Mule Skinner Blues" on the Grand Ole Opry. Their reputation, and bluegrass music's appeal, was formed.

Over the years Monroe's band was a virtual training school for future bluegrass legends, including Flatt and Scruggs, Reno and Smiley, Chubby Wise, Carter Stanley, Mac Wiseman, and Vassar Clements. Monroe's musical virtuosity attracted these young musicians, and his prickly personality forced them out on their own—a devil's bargain that kept bluegrass music fresh.

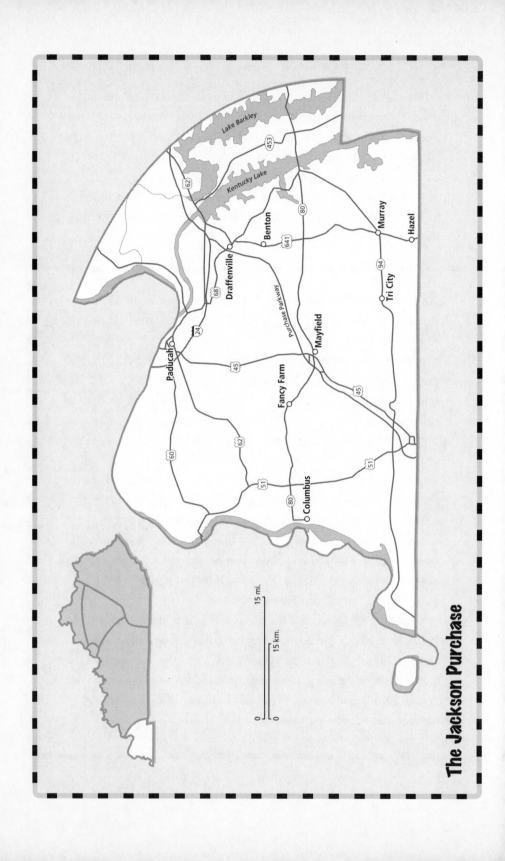

The Jackson Purchase

5

The Jackson Purchase

Many people wonder *why the western tip of Kentucky—an island-like land mass bounded by the Kentucky, Ohio, and Mississippi Rivers—is called the Jackson Purchase. It's very simple. Andrew Jackson bought it.*

The Purchase, as locals call it, wasn't added to the Kentucky map until more than two decades after statehood. That's when a commission headed by General Jackson, fresh off his triumphs in the War of 1812, negotiated a deal with the local Chickasaw Indians. Actually they could have called it the Shelby Purchase; the deal was brokered jointly by Jackson and former Kentucky Governor Isaac Shelby, and in all the documents Shelby's name is above Jackson's.

The treaty, signed on October 19, 1818, in northwestern Mississippi, gave the fledgling US government title to some 4,600 square miles of land that would be divvied up between Kentucky and Tennessee. In return the Chickasaw would be paid $300,000—$20,000 a year for fifteen years.

At least that's the way the schoolbooks tell it. That's because the schoolbooks didn't have all the facts. It seems that not all the Chickasaws wanted to sell their tribal land. In fact a lot of them didn't, and they threatened anyone who negotiated a treaty with the government. But Jackson and Shelby, by using, um, let's call it "backdoor financing," induced Chief Levi Colbert to sign over all the Chickasaw land in Kentucky and Tennessee. The Journal on Negotiations of the Chickasaw Treaty of 1818, *kept by the commission, puts it this way: "The*

Commissioners have been able to ascertain from the transactions of this week that an appeal becomes absolutely necessary to the avarice of the Chiefs."

To protect the tribesmen who signed the deal—and took the bribes—from retribution, Jackson ordered the treaty minutes be kept secret. And they were, for more than one hundred years. Those Chickasaw who couldn't be bribed were merely threatened. From the "secret" journal, this note: "General Jackson also told you that if you refuse to sell your claim that your white brothers would move on this land which is granted to them, and then your nation would have to apply to Congress for compensation, for if you refuse the good intentions of your father the President you cannot look to him for redress."

That $300,000 might not sound like much, but the land Jackson was buying wasn't much either; it was mostly uninhabited and, at the time, pretty uninhabitable. Still it was a bargain at what would be a little over three million in today's dollars.

Big Singing Day
Benton

In 1835 almost no one in America could read music. Heck, almost no one in America could read anything. So singing teacher William Walker devised a way to solve that: what he called "shaped notes," four shapes that told singers what notes to sing. He published a hymnal using his patented note system, *The Southern Harmony and Musical Companion: Containing a Choice Collection of Tunes, Hymns, Psalms, Odes, and Anthems; Selected from the Most Eminent Authors in the United States: Together with Nearly One Hundred New Tunes Which Have Never Before Been Published; Suited to Most of the Metres Contained in Watts's Hymns and Psalms, Mercer's Cluster, Dossey's Choice, Dover Selection, Methodist Hymn Book, and Baptist Harmony.* And despite the marathon title, it was a huge success.

Jump ahead to 1884. James R. Lemon, a newspaper publisher in Benton, organizes a Big Singing—an all-day community festival and homecoming with singing, singing, and more singing.

Jump ahead to today. The Big Singing is now the oldest indigenous music festival in the US. It doesn't draw the crowds it once did when special trains were chartered to bring people from all over the South. But 10,000 people is still quite a sight—and sound.

Big Singing Day is held each May on the grounds of the Marshall County Courthouse in Benton. For details call the Marshall County Chamber of Commerce at (270) 527-3585.

Tater Days
Benton

Kentucky has festivals for fruit, farm animals, and music. The state would not be complete without a festival honoring a side dish of some kind. Leave it to Benton to come to the rescue with the world's only— as far as we know—salute to the sweet potato.

★ ★

Benton is home of the Tater Day Festival—Tater Days, as it is known—a three-day event held on the weekend before the first Monday in April, honoring the sweet potato.

This form of spud was all the rage back in 1843 during court days, bringing in high bidding and trading values. Sweet potatoes grow well in Kentucky's hot, humid summer weather, making the tuber an easy cash crop.

To honor the spud there is a parade, carnival, and fiddling contest, as well as baking and canning contests. How many ways can you fix a sweet potato? At least enough to fill judging for three days.

For more information call (270) 527-7665 or visit the website www.explorekentuckylake.com/lakesarea/events/taterday.htm.

Kentucky in Missouri—Where the Mississippi Changed Course
Columbus

Kentuckians in the Mississippi River town of Columbus were as happy as a bug in a rug in 1811. Then on December 16 a natural disaster struck that would shake their world—literally. A massive earthquake hit about twenty-five miles away, in New Madrid, Missouri. That quake remains the most severe recorded earthquake to hit the continental US. New Madrid, a town of four hundred on the banks of the Mississippi, was totally destroyed. Three smaller—but not by much—quakes happened over the next seven weeks. This seismic activity, now referred to as the Great New Madrid Earthquake of 1811–1812, caused the Mississippi River to change course. Some locals claimed it even flowed backward for a few days.

When the mighty Mississippi shifted its shores, it left a part of what was then Livingston (now Hickman) County hanging—pinched off and shoved into Missouri. Over time Missourians noticed that a large chunk of Kentucky was on their side of the river, and in time they decided to stake a claim to it. The case wound up in the US Supreme Court, where in 1871 the justices ruled that despite its new location on the Missouri side of the Mississippi, the land would remain a part of Kentucky.

Kentucky Highway 58 takes you across the mighty Mississippi. Turn left on the first road in Missouri, Wolf Island Road, and you can drive into the once disputed chunk of land.

Dueling Oprys
Draffenville

Ever since George Hay introduced a new music program on Nashville radio in 1927 by telling his listeners they were no longer listening to Grand Opera but instead to "The Grand Ole Opry," "oprys" have popped up all over the south. There's the Carolina Opry (Myrtle Beach, South Carolina), the Virginia Opry (Clifton Forge, Virginia), even a Virginia-Kentucky Opry (Norton, Virginia).

In Kentucky we have two music halls that call themselves the Kentucky Opry. Perhaps we should dub them Kentucky Opry East and Kentucky Opry West. The eastern version in Prestonsburg is spotlighted in the Country Music Highway section of The Mountains chapter. The western version, which has been around two years longer than its eastern competition, is based in Draffenville, near Kentucky Lake. It's also the unofficial one. Prestonsburg's version receives funding from the Kentucky Arts Council. The one in Draffenville is supported solely by the paying customers. It started out in a Quonset hut with crowds of fewer than a couple of dozen neighbors. But the audience grew quickly, and in 1989 this Kentucky Opry moved into its own 540-seat theater.

Both oprys draw top-flight talent. A recent show in Draffenville featured The Grascals. Exile and Goose Creek Symphony have appeared in Prestonsburg. Ralph Stanley and the Clinch Mountain Boys appear regularly at both venues.

Kentucky Opry West is on Highway 641 in Draffenville, five miles south of the Kentucky Dam. Call (270) 527-3869 or (888) 459-8704.

Kentucky Opry East is held in the Mountain Arts Center, 50 Hal Rogers Drive, Prestonsburg. Call (888) MAC-ARTS (888-622-2787).

★ ★

Kentucky Opry West got there first on the Internet, too, with an eponymous website at www.kentuckyopry.com. Kentucky Opry East is now called Billie Jean Osborne's Kentucky Opry and can be found on the Internet at http://macarts.com/?page_id=162.

World's Largest One-Day Picnic
Fancy Farm

They say you can't even get elected dogcatcher in Kentucky if you don't speak at the annual Fancy Farm Picnic. That's what draws crowds of 15,000 and more—that and the barbecue. Cooks roast up more than nine tons of pork and mutton—a ton more than they cooked in 1984, the year the *Guinness World Record* people bestowed on Fancy Farm the title of World's Largest One-Day Picnic.

The Fancy Farm Picnic has been a must for political candidates of all stripes since before the Civil War. The fighting caused the event to be halted for a time, but it picked back up in 1880 and has been an annual event, the unofficial kickoff of the fall campaign, ever since.

Any candidate—local, state, or national—can speak, as long as he or she follows the rules: No speaking before 2:00 p.m. That gives everyone a chance to eat. And no speaking after 4:00 p.m. That gives everyone a chance to eat again. Oh yeah, and you have to speak next to the aptly named lyin' tree, a dead oak that got its name from the free flow of campaign promises beneath its branches. The tree was felled in 1974 by what is known around here as "a nonpartisan bolt of lightning."

The Fancy Farm Picnic is held the first Saturday in August at St. Jerome Church on Highway 339 in Fancy Farm. For more information call St. Jerome Church at (270) 623-8181, the Mayfield-Graves County Chamber of Commerce at (270) 247-6101, or visit www.fancyfarm picnic.org.

Ridin' That Train

The world has Sim Webb to thank for perpetuating the legend of Casey Jones. Webb rode with Jones as the train fireman the infamous night of the "Cannonball Express."

John Luther "Casey" Jones's legend begins in Cayce, Kentucky, the town that gave Jones his nickname. Jones became enamored with trains and railroads at an early age. When he was fifteen years old, Jones moved to Columbus, Kentucky, to work at the north terminal of the Mobile and Ohio (M&O) Railroad as a telegrapher. Soon he was promoted to brakeman on runs from Columbus to Jackson, Tennessee. In 1888 Jones left M&O and joined the Illinois Central Railroad, settling down with his wife in Jackson.

Life was good for Jones. In 1890 he was promoted to engineer and made runs from Jackson to Water Valley, Mississippi. In 1900 he was assigned to the Cannonball Express with runs from Memphis to Canton, Mississippi. The Cannonball Express was an assignment most engineers refused due to the high speeds and danger, but Jones loved his new duty.

At 3:52 a.m. on April 30, 1900, Jones was heading for Canton when three trains met at an intersection in Vaughan, Mississippi. This was not uncommon, and the trains attempted a "saw-by" that would have allowed Jones's express train to pass through. An air hose on one of the trains broke, however, and left four cars stranded on the mainline. Jones didn't see the cars until it was too late. He yelled at Webb to jump just before the trains collided. Casey stayed on trying to slow the train down as much as possible to save his passengers. He did—but he couldn't save himself. And thus was born the legend, "The Ballad of Casey Jones."

Webb passed the story of Casey Jones onto Wallace Saunders, who worked in the engine shop with the two, and Saunders wrote the song that told "the story about a brave engineer." The song was popularized by a couple of vaudeville performers, Siebert & Newton, who—legend has it—bought the song from Saunders for a pint of whiskey. Now there's the real legend of Casey Jones.

★ ★

Goin' Bananas

Fulton, Kentucky, was the reigning banana capital of the world until 1992—and I bet you thought it was South America! More than 70 percent of the world's banana shipments were sent through the tiny town. Bananas were loaded into refrigerator cars, "ice reefers" they were called, in New Orleans and shipped north by rail. The ice only lasted to Fulton, so the town became a stopping-off point where all the trains would stock up with a fresh supply of block ice to prevent the bananas from spoiling. Some of the trains were a mile-long with banana cars.

Wanting to celebrate their claim to fame, Fulton began the International Banana Festival in 1962. And what's a festival without a gimmick? Fulton's festival had several. First there was the banana hat contest, then the parade of fruit. And finally there was the world's largest banana pudding. Clearly the highlight of the festival, the pudding weighed more than one ton and served thousands.

But, alas, the banana industry isn't what it used to be, and Fulton lost its distinction as the Banana Capital—and its festival. After a thirty-year run, the International Banana Festival is no more. Now you have to go to a local restaurant if you want banana pudding.

Out with the New, In with the Old

Hazel

Hazel is the antiques capital of western Kentucky. So let's have a party! Held on the first Saturday in October, the Hazel Day Celebration—not a festival, mind you—celebrates everything old: old cars, old games, old people. There is an old-fashioned cakewalk, and a not-so-old-fashioned washer-pitching contest. No, not your GE model, the real old-fashioned washer things. Hearts begin to palpitate and beat just a little faster when the checkers tournament closes out the celebration.

The celebration has been going strong since 1990, with no signs of getting old yet. (Sorry for that!)

For more information on the Hazel Day Celebration, call (270) 492-8872 or visit www.hazelky.com/hazeldayactivities.htm.

The Procession That Never Moves
Mayfield

The world's slowest moving procession is located in Mayfield. Why is it so slow? Because it's a procession of statues—giant cement statues of the Wooldridge family, complete with lifelike dogs.

Dubbed "the strange procession that never moves," it features eighteen statues and adorns the entryway to the tomb of Colonel Henry Wooldridge, who was a horse trader. When he died in 1899, he commanded in his will that life-size exact replicas of his family be created to surround his tomb. The images of his aunts, sisters, uncles, parents, grandparents, and even the family dogs, Tow Head and Bob, are forever carved in stone for the world to see.

You might've seen the monuments before. They made an appearance in the 1989 Bruce Willis movie *In Country,* which was filmed in these parts.

The colonel is the only person actually entombed there. Unfortunately for the tourist, there's a fence surrounding the monument, thwarting would-be vandals—and would-be photographers.

The statues and procession can be found at Maplewood Cemetery on North Sixth Street in Mayfield. (There is no phone.)

★ ★

Bert & Bud's Dead Business
Murray

Say you weren't fortunate enough to have your leg blown off at the Battle of Perryville and die a horrible death from gangrene. Say you were just a run-of-the-mill Civil War reenactor who left this world by natural causes. That doesn't mean you can't ship out in Civil War style. You can. Just contact Bert & Bud, or have your nearest survivor do it for you.

Bert & Bud make caskets. But not just any caskets. Albert "Bert" Sperath and Roy "Bud" Davis make custom caskets. They say your

Rest in peace your way.
COURTESY OF ROY DAVIS, BERT & BUD'S VINTAGE COFFINS

casket is your final opportunity to make a profound statement about your life—as their ads promise, "To say, 'This is how I want to be remembered.'"

You can be remembered in a simple wooden coffin or something a little more elaborate, a little more personal. After all, who wants to make that final journey in an assembly-line casket? And if you enjoyed Civil War reenacting in life, why not enjoy it in death, too, with a Civil War–era casket.

Bert & Bud promise their coffins are "built one at a time to the measurements, specifications, and tastes of each customer." You may remember the slogan from your high-school yearbook. On the ad for the local funeral home, some funnyman had added: "We're the last to let you down." That's Bert & Bud.

For more information, call Bert & Bud at (270) 753-9279 or visit them on the web at www.vintagecoffins.com.

Marconi, Schmoni—Radio Was Born Here

Murray

Poor Nathan Stubblefield. He invented radio and didn't even get a lousy T-shirt, much less any mention in the history books. Of course it didn't help any that Nathan was secretive, suspicious, and stubborn. Nor did it help that he died in 1929 in his shack of starvation, leading people to think of him less as a genius than as a mad genius.

It all dates to 1892, when Stubblefield demonstrated his Stubble-field's Black Box to a friend named Rainey T. Wells. He handed Wells one black box and told him to walk away. When Wells got a couple of hundred yards down the path, he heard a distinct noise coming from his box. "Hello, Rainey," the voice said. Let's let Rainey pick up the story. "I jumped a foot and said to myself, 'This fellow is fooling me. He has wires someplace.'" Rainey kept moving, but the voice kept following. "All the while he kept talking to me . . . but there were no wires, I tell you."

★ ★

It would be ten years before Stubblefield was ready for a public demonstration, and he chose the steps of the Calloway County Courthouse. He set up one box on the steps and directed his son, Bernard, to set up a second box some two hundred feet away. He and Bernard then began conducting a conversation as if they were standing next to each another, much to the astonishment of a large throng gathered around. He later demonstrated the device at a distance of one mile for an amazed *St. Louis Post-Dispatch* reporter, who listened as Bernard played the harmonica and sang.

Stubblefield made an attempt at marketing his invention, but the company he partnered with, the Philadelphia-based Wireless Telephone Company of America, turned out to be a scam set up for the purpose of selling stock, not developing a product. Bitter, Stubblefield retired to his shack and wasn't heard from again until his body was found by a neighbor.

There is much debate about what Stubblefield actually invented. A modern analysis of his patents and the historical record doesn't fully support a claim as the Father of Radio. But almost no one disputes that son Bernard was the first person to broadcast music to an audience, even if it was an audience of one, the St. Louis reporter.

A stone memorial on the campus of Murray State College commemorates his legend. "Here, in 1902, Nathan Stubblefield (1860–1928), inventor of radio, broadcast and received human voice by wireless."

Working Stiff—Kentucky's Mummy
Paducah

Speedy Atkins was just a working stiff, a messenger in a tobacco company, when he went fishing on that fateful day in 1928. He fell asleep on the bank, tumbled into the Ohio River, and drowned.

When authorities could find no next of kin to the lifelong bachelor, they turned his body over to funeral home attendant A. Z. Hamock, who worked at Watkins Undertaking Parlor, the city's only African-American funeral home, for a pauper's burial. But Hamock decided instead to experiment with an embalming fluid he had been developing. The result turned Speedy into something that looked like a wooden statue.

Hamock was so taken with the result that he decided that rather than bury Speedy, he would put him on display in the funeral home. And that's where Speedy resided for almost three-quarters of a century. In death the anonymous messenger became famous, appearing on a number of national TV shows, including *That's Incredible*, *Ripley's Believe It Or Not!*, and *A Current Affair*.

Hamock's widow, Velma, decided she was going to bury old Speedy in 1991 on her late husband's one-hundredth birthday, but you know how things are. She didn't get around to it until May 1994. And that's where Speedy is today.

Speedy's grave is in the Maplelawn Cemetery, 1335 North Thirteenth Street. For information call (270) 442-2538.

A Stitch in Time

Paducah

In Kentucky quilts are quilts; they are handmade blankets that folks use to keep themselves warm. But in other parts of the country, quilts are collectibles, a form of folk art. We didn't realize that for a long time. So quilt "dealers" were coming into the state, buying up our quilts, carting them off, and selling them for three, four, ten times what they bring here.

We woke up to that fact in the 1980s and began treating quilts for what they are: gorgeous examples of handwork. And thus in 1991 was born the Museum of the American Quilter's Society, a place to house a representative collection while photographing and documenting many others. It's the largest museum of its kind in the world. Why Paducah? Because the founders of the American Quilter's Society, Meredith and Bill Schroeder, live here.

The permanent collection at the museum features quilts from all over, not just Kentucky. If you're lucky enough to be in the area in late

★ ★

April, you can enjoy the annual quilt show; more than four hundred quilts are on display, competing for $80,000 in prizes.

Quilts . . . they're not just for bedtime anymore.

The museum is at 215 Jefferson Street. Except for holidays, it's open year-round Monday through Saturday 10:00 a.m. to 5:00 p.m., and on Sunday afternoon from 1:00 to 5:00 p.m., April through October. Admission is free. For more information call (270) 442-8856 or visit www.quiltmuseum.org.

Home of the Atomic Bomb

Perhaps you thought it was Los Alamos—or Oak Ridge. Ah, it's all in the wording: not "Birthplace of," but "Home of."

The atomic bomb wasn't invented in Paducah. But since 1952 Paducah has been home to an operating uranium-enrichment facility. And since 2001 it has been home to the only operating uranium enrichment facility in the US. What does that mean? It means if you're afraid of acquiring an eerie green glow, you might not want to move here. Not that any locals have a green glow, but this is the place where radioactive uranium is enriched so that it can fuel, oh, a bomb. They don't do that anymore and haven't produced any bomb-grade enriched uranium since 1962. We have treaties and all. Now Paducah produces fuel for nuclear power plants.

Why Paducah? Some think it might have something to do with the fact that when the contract was awarded in 1950, the vice president of the US was none other than Alben Barkley, a native of nearby Graves County who had once practiced law in Paducah.

The Paducah Gaseous Diffusion Plant is located some ten miles west of town near the Ohio River in McCracken County. Yes, there's a big fence.

* *

Lady Sells the Booze
Paducah

The dirty-looking fellows who knocked at Lucille Edwards's door in 2001 wanted to buy some whiskey. Without even asking for ID, the Paducah woman retrieved the liquor, took their money, and was heading back to washing dishes. That's when the thirsty souls revealed their true identities. They were undercover McCracken County Sheriff's deputies—and Miss Lucille was under arrest for "bootlegging."

Edwards later pleaded guilty to the charges and was fined $500 and sentenced to 120 days of home incarceration, not a bad deal for a bootlegger who sold whiskey out the back door of her house. It was Edwards's second offense, but the judge had mercy after her lawyer explained she was frail. "She never leaves the home anyway," he told the judge. The judge also considered another factor in Edwards's story. She was eighty-two years old and a great-grandmother!

Monkey Man
Paducah

You've heard of the infamous Scopes Monkey Trial. It was held in Dayton, Tennessee, in 1925 as a challenge to our sister state's law against teaching evolution. But do you know who the Scopes of Scopes Monkey Trial was? He was Kentucky native John Thomas Scopes, a substitute teacher who was born in Paducah and graduated from the University of Kentucky in Lexington.

Scopes was a twenty-four-year-old football coach and science teacher when he happened to stop by Robinson's Drug Store in Dayton one May morning in 1925. One of the regulars at the store, George Rappelyea, was reading a *Chattanooga Daily Times* story about Tennessee's new law, the Butler Act, which forbid the teaching of evolution in the public schools. The story noted that the American Civil Liberties Union was looking to fund a challenge to the law. Rappelyea thought that just might be what sleepy little Dayton needed—a big show trial that would bring attention, and tourists, to town.

Quintessential Kentuckians

Irvin S. Cobb

Kentucky humorist Irvin Cobb, whose glory years on the literary scene were the first third of the twentieth century, was a writer and storyteller known the world over for his sly wit and good Kentucky sense. The short, portly Cobb, with his ever-present cigar, was a fixture on the New York literary scene. He wrote sixty books and more than three hundred short stories, sixteen of which were turned into films, including the 1933 Cary Grant film *Woman Accused,* the 1934 Will Rogers comedy *Judge Priest,* and the 1953 John Ford film *The Sun Shines Bright.* His success made him the highest-paid writer of his day, favorably compared to Mark Twain and Edgar Allan Poe.

He once quipped, "A good storyteller is a person who has a good memory and hopes other people haven't." Commenting on the nation's capital, he noted, "Washington is a good place to go crazy because it will not be noticed." His most prescient quote was this one: "If writers were good businessmen, they'd have too much sense to be writers."

But times, and tastes in humor, change; today his books are out of print and his words are mostly found in a few works of familiar quotes. Even those in his hometown of Paducah only know him, if at all, as the namesake for the landmark Hotel Irvin S. Cobb, now the Irvin Cobb Apartments, or the namesake of a local highway, Irvin Cobb Drive.

Rappelyea summoned Scopes over. Under questioning, the young Kentuckian admitted he taught biology for only two weeks, filling in for the ailing regular teacher. He wasn't even sure what he had covered in his ten days. "We reviewed for final exams, as best I remember."

That was good enough for Rappelyea. And thus was born one of the most famous trials of the twentieth century with, as its defendant, poor John Scopes, who in all likelihood never taught a single sentence of evolutionary biology.

John Scopes died in 1970 at age seventy and is buried in Section 7, Lot #104 of the Oak Grove Cemetery in Paducah. The cemetery is at 1613 Park Avenue. For information call (270) 444-8532. While you're visiting Oak Grove, you might search out the headstone for Dollie the mule. That's right, a mule in a people cemetery. Dollie was interred in Oak Grove in 1897 after sixteen years of pulling the local fire wagon.

Open All Night
Paducah

In other cities they're just concrete walls—gray and imposing, but not friendly. But Paducah has taken its downtown floodwalls—a necessity considering the city's location on the Ohio River—and turned them into art, inviting and appealing.

The Paducah Wall-to-Wall Murals project began in 1986 as part of a downtown revitalization project. Now there are forty-eight images that tell the city's story from the steamboat era to a modern motorcycle gang. All the murals were painted by nationally known Louisiana muralist Robert Dafford, who arrives in town every year to add to his project.

There are bus tours of the murals, but the best way to see them is up close and personal, studying the depth of focus in each panel and then reading about it in the interpretive panels that are in front of each section.

The murals have led Paducah to create a unique event, The Festival of Murals, which features living tableaus: actors in period costumes

★ ★

standing in front of the murals and acting out the events depicted on the wall.

Best of all, the mural scenes are open all night.

The murals are on Broadway Street, near South First.

For more information call (800) PADUCAH (800-723-8224) or visit the city's website at www.paducah-tourism.org.

Road Map to Heaven
Tri City

Want to know how to get to heaven? Lesley Murdock can tell you. Even though he died in 1979, Murdock is still offering a road map at his mausoleum.

Murdock, who founded Paradise Friendly Home, the only orphanage in Graves County, specified that his interment site include his instructions—heavy on scripture from the Gospel of John—detailing the road to grace. Murdock and his wife are the only ones buried at the site.

There used to be letters atop the mausoleum that spelled out STOP AND SEE A ROADMAP TO HEAVEN. That's been removed. But there is a plaque that reads ROADMAP TO HEAVEN—WHAT MUST I DO TO BE SAVED? It provides a six-step answer—but if I include that here, then there's no point in visiting the gravesite.

Tri City is at the intersection of Highway 94 and Highway 97.

6

Northern Kentucky

Northern Kentucky is *almost indistinguishable from southern Ohio, thanks to their shared cultural center, Cincinnati. But there is a difference. The Cincinnati side is known for its conservatism. Mark Twain once said, "When the end of the world comes, I want to be in Cincinnati—it is always ten years behind the times."*

While the north side of the Ohio River, southern Ohio, has given us such wholesome icons as Doris Day and Roy Rogers, the south side—that would be northern Kentucky—is where porn magnate Larry Flynt was born and a pre-tabloid TV Jerry Springer was involved in a sex scandal (he paid a prostitute with a check). It's a little rougher trade on this side of the bridge.

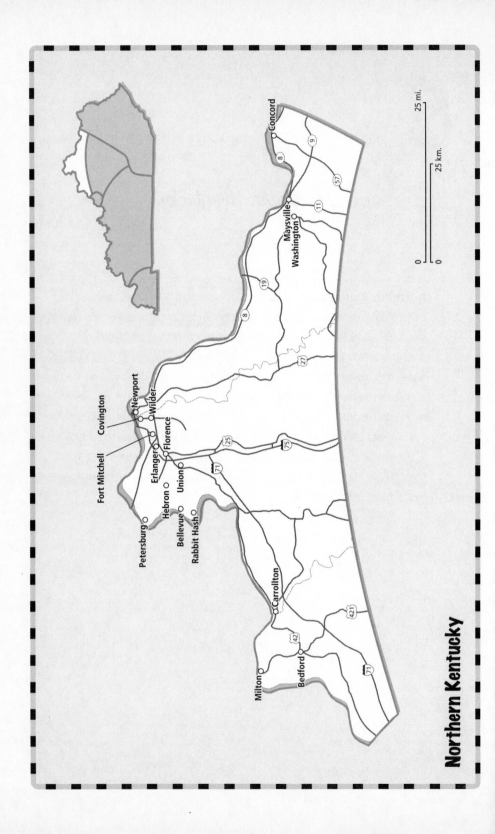

Northern Kentucky

Kentucky Bigfoot
Bedford

Owen Powell was the first person to report it. The creature, more than six feet tall and covered with pitch-black hair—"not quite a dog, a panther, or a bear"—was in his hog pen. He sent his dogs after it; not just any old porch dogs, but a German shepherd and a collie. The beast beat them back, sending them whimpering to their master.

It was June 3, 1962, and soon Trimble County Sheriff Clem Curtis began receiving other reports of this "Thing," as the locals called it. It was agitating the hogs and stirring up the dogs. That week, reports continued to trickle in of strange animal deaths. There were numerous other spottings. Then, on June 13, a footprint the size of a human hand with four stubby toes was found.

Hanover College zoologist Dr. J. Daniel Webster thought that it was a dog's print, but agreed that no dog could create the havoc this "Thing" was wreaking, climbing in barn windows and doing unspeakable acts to calves and heifers.

The sheriff's department put on an all-out man, er, beasthunt on June 18, 1962, but found neither hide nor hair of the beast. The Thing was never spotted again. Four decades later they still argue in Trimble County about what this mysterious creature was. Was it a dog—or was it really Bigfoot?

Most of the spottings were on Kidwell Road. The Cliffs, where much of the beasthunt focused, is one mile below Hanover, Indiana, on the Kentucky side of the Ohio River.

★ ★

Forgotten Fourth—Tinker to Evers to Chance to . . .
Bellevue

It is the most famous infield in baseball history, immortalized by Franklin P. Adams in a bit of doggerel he published in the *New York World* in 1910:

These are the saddest of possible words,
Tinker-to-Evers-to-Chance.
Trio of Bear Cubs fleeter than birds,
Tinker-to-Evers-to-Chance.

Joe Tinker, Johnny Evers, and Frank Chance were, respectively, the shortstop, second baseman, and first baseman of the Chicago Cubs. You don't have to be a student of baseball to recognize that something—or someone—is missing: Harry Steinfeldt. Good old Harry was the third baseman for that great Cubs team but was sadly neglected by Adams in his famous poem and ended up the answer to a trivia question: Who was the "other" infielder in the Cubs' famous Tinker-to-Evers-to-Chance infield of the early 1900s?

Steinfeldt was every bit the player that Tinker, Evers, and Chance were. In 1906, the year the Cubs set a major league record by winning 116 games, he led the National League in hits and RBIs and was the top-fielding third baseman. Tinker led shortstops in fielding that season; neither Chance nor Evers led at their positions. Steinfeldt's bad luck was that he just didn't happen to be part of the Cubs' respected double-play combination.

Right after Adams's poem was published, Steinfeldt had his worst season ever. Whether it had anything to do with being neglected in the poem, we will never know. But it began a downward spiral that culminated on August 17, 1914, when he was killed in a bar fight in Bellevue, just three years after retiring, at the age of thirty-seven.

Gathering of the Clans

Carrollton

Is your last name McTavish? Or McCoy or MacVicar or any of the hundreds of other Scottish surnames that populate the phonebooks? Then you may want to rearrange your vacation schedule and meet up with some of your long-lost relatives in a most unlikely place: Kentucky.

Kentucky is not known for its Scottish population; German and Irish, yes, but not Scottish. Louisville has its Germantown and was home for many years to the *Irish-American* newspaper. But we have our Scottish clans, too, so to speak. And every May they gather at General Butler State Resort Park in Carrollton for the Kentucky Scottish Weekend: two days of Scottish games, good eats, and great fun.

Real clansmen don't wear pants.
COURTESY OF KENTUCKYTOURISM.COM

★ ★

The big crowds assemble for the games. These are not your ordinary Olympic events. These are brute strength games, like the twenty-two-pound hammer throw, the fifty-six-pound weight toss, and the most challenging of all, the caber toss, which involves hoisting a 175-pound tree trunk. On Saturday you can watch the pros, then on Sunday you can try the events yourself—on scaled down versions, of course.

For those who prefer a bit more grace with their athletics, there's Scottish country dancing throughout the day, both Saturday and Sunday. The highlight of the weekend is the Ceilidh (KAY-lee), a Saturday night sing-along that blends voices with a pipe band.

For information visit www.kyscottishweekend.org or write Kentucky Scottish Weekend, Inc., PO Box 11441, Cincinnati, OH 45211-0441.

Staying on Track
Carrollton

We love our trains in Kentucky. There's the Kentucky Railway Museum in New Haven and My Old Kentucky Dinner Train in Bardstown; the Elkhorn City Railroad Museum in Elkhorn City and the David A. Zegeer Coal-Railroad Museum in Jenkins; and the Bluegrass Railroad Museum in Versailles and this festival and swap meet for toy train aficionados in Carrollton.

We especially love our toy trains. Witness the Toy Train Festival, which attracts grown-up little boys from all over the country. You'll see everything from classic Lionel models to modern favorites like Thomas—and a swap meet like no other. At the end of the weekend many of the train enthusiasts head to nearby La Grange to watch the train go through the middle of the city. Now that's excitement.

For information on the Toy Train show, call (502) 743-5414.

Population 35—and Shrinking

Concord

If you're old enough to recognize the names George Maharis and Martin Milner, then you know about Concord, the first stop for Maharis and Milner on their 1960s TV drama *Route 66*. The first episode of the show was filmed in Concord, and the tiny town has been grateful ever since. But all that publicity couldn't turn the tide. Concord has been withering on the vine for more than half a century, and in the latest census it finally fell to the bottom: It is officially Kentucky's smallest town.

There may be communities with a smaller population than thirty-five, but none is a bona-fide city, incorporated and a dues-paying member of the Kentucky League of Cities. Concord has a mayor and a town council; in fact the governing group comprises 20 percent of the town's residents.

Concord is shrinking despite the fact that it now has its own grocery store, Mary McClurg's Concord Little Country Store, which reopened in the mid-1990s. (McClurg told the Associated Press that she has to sell everything from foodstuffs to antiques to stay afloat; business is best when there's a funeral in town.)

In the 1990 census Concord had sixty-five residents. It shrank by more than half in the next ten years. Ah, but it had its glory days. When the town was incorporated in 1830, it boasted three hotels, a boarding house, a drugstore, a sawmill, a doctor, and a lawyer.

Things have been downhill in the Lewis County community since the flood of '84—that's 1884—swept away most of First Street. The famous Ohio River flood of 1937 swallowed the rest of that lane—twenty-eight houses—and sent the town into a downward spiral.

Aside from McClurg's store there's not much else left in town: two churches and City Hall. That small population means a small tax base. When the city coffers are bare, Mayor Lovell Polley dips into his own pocket to pay the City Hall electric bill.

★ ★

Jesus (Could've) Slept Here
Covington

You don't have to go all the way to the Holy Land to see the tomb where Jesus was buried. You can visit Covington and see the only replica in this country. The Garden of Hope is modeled on Jerusalem's Garden Tomb, one of several Middle Eastern sites that are considered possibilities for Jesus's final resting place.

The idea for the tomb came from local TV evangelist Morris H. Coers, who visited the real site in 1938 and returned to America determined to build a duplicate. It took him almost a quarter century, but the Garden of Hope was officially dedicated on Easter Sunday 1960.

A renowned replica.

Sadly, the Reverend Coers didn't live to see the formal dedication; he died two months earlier.

The Reverend Coers was a stickler for details. He contracted with Solomon Mattar, caretaker of Jerusalem's Garden Tomb, to provide drawings of the Israeli site. Coers even flew Mattar in to put on the finishing touches. The garden includes stones imported from the Jordan River, the Wailing Wall, and Solomon's Temple. When it was finished, the Reverend Coers proclaimed the replica so accurate that even the interior echo sounded the same as the original.

But without its benefactor, the Garden of Hope fell on hard times. In the mid-1990s an anonymous benefactor paid off the Garden's debt, and a committee from Coers's old church, Immanuel Baptist, oversaw a renovation that has the garden back to its original grandeur.

The Garden of Hope is located at 699 Edgecliff Drive just off Sixteenth Street. For information call (859) 491-1777.

The Big Picture
Covington

If you get up close, where you can't see the surrounding city, and squint, it's like a miniature Notre Dame. Except, of course, that no amount of urban renewal could make you think that Covington is Paris.

The cathedral does have its own claim to world fame: It houses the largest hand-blown stained-glass church window in the world. The cathedral's north transept window, which depicts the fifth-century Ecumenical Council of Ephesus that proclaimed Mary as the Mother of God, is sixty-seven feet high and twenty-four feet wide. All told, the church has eighty-two stained-glass windows.

The church is actually a copy of three famous French chapels: The exterior comes from the Abbey Church of Saint-Denis in Paris; the three-tiered interior walls are copied from Notre Dame de Chartres; and the facade is a one-third-scale replica of Cathedral de Notre Dame in Paris.

The ultimate suncatcher.

★ ★

The cathedral is one of thirty-five minor basilicas in the US and is home to the Roman Catholic Diocese of Covington. And here's a secret: The cathedral has never been completed; construction stopped in 1915.

The Cathedral Basilica of the Assumption is located at 1140 Madison Avenue. For more information visit www.covcathedral.com.

Father of Scouting Fathered in Kentucky
Covington

Daniel Carter Beard, or "Uncle Dan" as he is known to millions of men and young boys around the world, was born and raised in Covington—scout's honor!

Born in 1851, Beard, the founding father of the American Boy Scouts, grew up camping and hiking in the wooded areas of Kentucky. He was deeply fascinated by tales of Daniel Boone and frontiersmen—he was only fifty or so years removed from those frontier days—spending hours re-creating their experiences.

Beard was an environmentalist at heart, although he did set out to pursue a career in civil engineering and surveying. His passions were refocused, though, when outdoor and nature magazines began publishing illustrations he had drawn. Beard left engineering and never looked back.

The Boy Scouts were an organization formed in England. Stemming in part from his admiration for what the Brits were doing in teaching environmentalism to children, and in part from a desire to pass on his childhood experiences to kids who might not have access to nature and the outdoors, Beard formed the Boy Scouts of America in 1910. He also served as the first National Commissioner of the Boy Scouts, designed the uniforms, served as president of the Campfire Girls, formed the Society of the Sons of Daniel Boone, and wrote what is considered to be the definitive environmentalist manual, *The American Boy's Handy Book,* which has been in continuous publication for one hundred years. Whew! The *Handy Book* continues to be the bible of the Boy Scouts to this day.

★ ★

Beard also illustrated many books, including the first edition of Mark Twain's *A Connecticut Yankee in King Arthur's Court.* Mount Beard, adjoining Mount McKinley, is named for him. Scout's honor.

Daniel Carter Beard Environmental Center is at 322 East Third Street in Covington. For information call (859) 261-3882.

Brick Shot—John Wooden's Only Coaching Failure

John Wooden was the greatest coach in the history of collegiate basketball. There's no argument even. He won more college basketball championships, ten, than any other coach. That's more than his closest rivals combined. His UCLA teams were legendary. They once won eighty-eight games in a row and had a stretch of seven consecutive NCAA tournament championships between 1967 and 1973.

But he wasn't always so successful. In fact, when Wooden started his coaching career at Dayton High School, his teams were not very good. He coached only two seasons there, but his record was a middling 21–14, including a losing season—a reported 8–9—in 1933–34. It was his only losing season in more than forty years of coaching.

In Wooden's defense he was a little busy those two years, coaching all of the school's athletic teams while teaching English and phys ed and adapting to his newlywed status—all on $150 a month. He left Dayton after the 1934 season to coach at South Bend Central in his native Indiana. In eleven years coaching high school basketball, his teams won 218 games while losing only forty-two. One-third of his losses were those two years in Kentucky.

Gotta Get Some Goetta

Erlanger

If the waitress at Colonial Cottage asks if you want goetta, don't respond, "Do I want to getta what?" That's not what she's asking. She's asking if you want the local specialty, goetta, with your meal.

Goetta is a sausage made by combining ground pork and beef with oats and seasonings. The dish was created by Cincinnati's German immigrant community in the nineteenth century as a breakfast dish, often served with eggs and pancakes.

While goetta was created in Cincinnati, its most successful purveyors are here in Kentucky. Most commercial goetta is manufactured by Covington's Glier's Specialty Haus. And the restaurant for goetta is the Colonial Cottage, where the most popular dish is goetta and eggs. The Cottage has been serving up goetta since 1933.

If you just can't "goetta" enough goetta, you'll want to make plans to attend the annual Goettafest held in late summer at Newport, Kentucky's Riverfront Levee. In 2005, 80,000 goetta-lovers packed the Levee to sample some thirty different goetta dishes, including the goetta Reuben, the goetta omelet, the goetta calzone, and goetta-stuffed mushrooms. And yes, there's even a goettaburger.

The Colonial Cottage is located at 3140 Dixie Highway in Erlanger. Dixie Highway is US Highway 42. Take exit Interstate 71 south on State Road 236, then take US Highway 42 north. Phone (859) 341-4498.

Glier's Specialty Haus is at 533 Goetta Place in Covington, just a block east of Interstate 75. Phone (859) 291-1800, or visit www .goetta.com. The website for Goettafest is www.goettafest.com.

Fantasy Suites

Florence

In Florence you can visit the Old West, a stock car race, and the 1950s— all without leaving the hotel grounds. Sound like a fantasy? That's what it's supposed to be. The Wildwood Inn offers a half dozen or so fantasy suites for visitors who want more than just a clean bed and cable TV.

★ ★

For cowboys there's the Western Suite, with a poker table, an Old West–style bar, and an iron bed. For authenticity you pump your water; there are no spigots.

For Neanderthals there's the Cave Suite, with stalactites and stalag-mites and a waterfall in the spa.

For sailors there's the Nautical Suite, with sleeping quarters in a boat.

For lovers, there's the Cupid Suite, complete with a heart-shaped spa and a room decor that's heavy on the red.

For a small price you and your honey can rev your engines in the racecar room.

★ ★

Sleep like an Egyptian. A room fit for a king—King Tut, that is—awaits you at the Wildwood Inn.

For NASCAR fans, there's the Pit Spa, with a racecar in the middle of the room and a Craftsman tool-caddy dresser.

And for fans of the 1950s there's the Happy Days Suite, with a Cadillac bed (honest, the bed is inside a 1959 Caddy convertible), a ten-cent soft drink machine, and an Elvis figurine that shakes its hips to "Jail House Rock."

Yes, fantasy is the Wildwood's stock-in-trade. If you just want a clean bed and cable TV, the Wildwood has one hundred regular rooms, too.

The Wildwood Inn is at 7809 US Highway 42, just off Interstate 75 at exit 180. Call (859) 371-6300 or visit www.wildwood-inn.com for more information.

★ ★

World's Smallest Church

Fort Mitchell

Perhaps you remember the *Newhart* episode where Bob Newhart's character, Dick Loudon, was host of a local TV talk show and the day's guest had been billed as the world's smallest horse. "How do

Services in this church are standing room only.

you know he's the world's smallest horse?" Dick earnestly asked the owner. "Well, look at him," the cowboy replied.

You'll have to accept on faith, as it were, that the Monte Casino Chapel in Fort Mitchell is the world's smallest church. But look at it! It's six feet by nine feet, just enough room for two worshippers. And that's a snug fit.

The chapel, on the campus of Thomas More College, has been featured in *Ripley's Believe It Or Not!* as the world's smallest church, so what more validation could you want?

Why would someone build a church this small? The chapel was originally constructed as a sort of convenient prayer station for monks who worked in the vineyards that once stood here.

The world's smallest church, the Monte Casino Chapel, is located on the campus of Thomas More College. The college is on Turkey Foot Road, just south of Interstate 275.

Dummies for Dummies
Fort Mitchell

Gone are the days of Ed Sullivan and Steve Allen, and gone with them are the regular national venues for "vents." Vent is short for ventriloquist, and in the days of Sullivan's *Toast of the Town,* performers who could throw their voices were a regular attraction. Now about the only place to enjoy the art is at Vent Haven, the only museum in America dedicated exclusively to ventriloquism.

Vent Haven is home to nearly six hundred dummies—"dolls," vents prefer to call them—some of them more than a century old. The museum was the brainchild of Cincinnati businessman W. S. Berger, whose actor-father introduced him to the craft when he was a boy. Berger didn't get serious about collecting vent memorabilia until after his retirement from the presidency of the Cambridge Tile Co. in 1947. But when he got serious, boy, did he get serious. In addition to the variety of dummies, there are films, sheet music, props, and an eight-hundred-book library of ventriloquism manuals and joke books.

★ ★

Among the inductees to the museum's Vent's Hall of Fame are Edgar Bergen, Shari Lewis, Paul Winchell, and Senor Wences. The museum doesn't have the most famous vent doll of all time, Bergen's Charlie McCarthy—that one is in the Smithsonian —but it does have a detailed replica made especially for Vent Haven with the permission of Bergen's widow, Frances.

Vent Haven, 33 West Maple Avenue, is open only during the summer and only by appointment. The highlight of the museum's season is the annual international ConVENTion at the nearby Drawbridge Estate. For information call (859) 341-0461 or visit www.venthaven.com.

Cincinnati, Kentucky
Hebron

Lunken Airport, Cincinnati, Ohio's international airport, is actually located in Kentucky. Oh, it wasn't always in Kentucky. At one time it was actually in Cincinnati, sitting on the city's eastern edge. But after the infamous 1937 Ohio River flood swamped the site, it became known as "Sunken Lunken," and Cincinnati began looking for a new site for its airport. It found it on a plateau thirteen miles south of town, and in 1947 the first commercial airliner, a flight from Cleveland, landed at what was then Boone County Airport.

A 1948 flood at Sunken Lunken cinched the deal, and Cincinnati's namesake airport has been in Kentucky ever since. And it's been a good deal. In 2001 the Cincinnati/Northern Kentucky International Airport was named Best Airport in the United States for passenger service and convenience in a survey by the International Air Transport Association.

The airport is located just off Interstate 275, west of Interstate 75. For information visit www.cincinnati-oh.gov/transeng/pages/-7207-/.

Population Center of 1880

The exact center of the population of the United States in 1880 was located in Kentucky. In fact it was located pretty much where the Cincinnati Airport is today. Of course the population wasn't all that great in 1880—just 49,371,340, give or take a few souls.

What's that? You understand geographic center but what is the population center? Here's how demographers explained it to me. Let's say everyone in the entire country weighed the same, say 150 pounds. Then have everyone go home and sit for just one second. Now peel up the country and put it on a needle. You'll have to move the needle around, but when you get it to that one spot where the country balances, that's the population center.

When they took the 1880 census, that balancing spot was in Hebron, Kentucky—where planes land today.

The center of the nation, circa 1880.

First Town Named for Our First President

Maysville

No, the first president wasn't named Mays. It's just that Washington, Kentucky, is now a part of Maysville.

George Washington wasn't even president when the town was named in his honor in 1780. He was still a blue-collar general, fighting the British up and down the East Coast, trying to win independence for the Colonies. Cornwallis didn't surrender until the next year, and Washington didn't become president until 1789. By that time, his namesake town, home to 119 log cabins, was the second largest town in the state. Okay, technically Kentucky wasn't a state yet either. But Washington was the second largest town in the area that would become the state of Kentucky.

So the townspeople jumped the gun a little, hoping that the thriving little town would be named the capital of the soon-to-be United States. It didn't happen, of course. In fact it was probably a little cheeky to name a town for a rebel general while a war was still going on.

Washington did become a happening village for a time. It was a fashion center in the last years of the eighteenth century, with twenty stores, ten mechanics shops, three churches, and two—count 'em, two—taverns. Despite the town's whistling and pulling up its skirt for attention, it never got the notice it wanted from the nation's father. George Washington never even slept here.

Rosemary Clooney House

Maysville

Rosemary Clooney became a big star in Hollywood, but she never lost her small-town roots in Kentucky. While she was becoming famous for appearing in *White Christmas* alongside Bing Crosby and lending her voice to the jazz hit *Come On-A My House,* privately Clooney was fighting bipolar disorder, depression, and drug addiction. In the 1980s, a healthy Clooney purchased a riverfront home in Maysville to be closer to her family in Augusta, Kentucky.

★ ★

She shuffled between Hollywood and this home until her death in 2002. Shortly after Clooney's passing, former Miss America 2000, Heather French Henry, and her husband, Steve Henry, the former lieutenant governor of Kentucky, bought the house. The Clooney family asked the Henrys to open the house to the public as a museum. The Henrys obliged and now manage the nonprofit Rosemary Clooney House. The museum includes memorabilia chronicling Clooney's life. There is also an exhibit dedicated to her nephew George Clooney and his life in Augusta.

The Rosemary Clooney House is located at 106 Riverside Drive in Maysville. For more information check out the website at www .rosemaryclooney.org.

A Sentimental Journey
Maysville

What, no hot air balloon rides or 5K runs or antique tractors? This unique festival is an annual celebration of the fact that Rosemary Clooney could sing (something nephew George Clooney can't do; his voice was dubbed in for *O Brother Where Art Thou*). It's music, music, and more music.

Each September big-band legend Clooney would return to her hometown of Maysville from her Hollywood home for a concert to benefit the "Rescue the Russell" restoration project. The Russell is the Russell Theatre, a defunct movie house in downtown Maysville. The Russell had a special place in Clooney's heart. It's where she had the world premiere for her first film, *The Stars Are Singing,* in 1953.

Clooney and musical guests (one year it was Michael Feinstein, another it was daughter-in-law Debby Boone) would perform under the stars in the middle of Maysville's historic district. Clooney died in 2002, but the show goes on.

For ticket information—the event includes dinner—call (606) 564-9411.

A Yard Sale with No End in Sight

In the pecking order of bargain hunting, it's the lowest—a notch below the flea market and several rungs down from the antiques auction. But the yard sale has its devotees, and every August they gather on a 450-mile stretch of US Highway 127 that runs from Covington all the way to Gadsden in northern Alabama to find those ultimate bargains.

And bargains there are: You can find anything from an antique oil painting to a used rake. There are car parts, music tapes, antiques, folk art, serious art, crafts—well, everything. There are as many different types of merchandise as there are vendors, and there are a lot of those—an estimated 3,500 tables and tents alongside the road.

It's a four-day yard sale, and veterans of the trek say there's no possible way to cover it all in four days. That's why the truly serious sneak out on Sunday, four days before the actual kickoff, and scour the merchandise even while the merchants are carting it out of the basement. The idea for the highway sale started with former Fentress County, Tennessee, official Mike Walker. He just wanted to get travelers off the interstate and into his county to do a little shopping. But the yard sale quickly took on a life of its own, jumping from a few dozen roadside vendors to a few thousand.

Traffic slows to a standstill in the more congested areas. That's because the event typically draws 20,000 cars. That's 20,000 more than the highway normally carries. If you can't find it at this yard sale, you don't need it.

The Fentress County (Tennessee) Chamber of Commerce coordinates the event. For information call (931) 879-9948 or visit www.127sale.com.

A Pink Flamingo and More

Milton

Business is not what it used to be on US Highway 421 at the Kentucky-Indiana border—surely not what it was back in the 1950s and '60s, when Route 421 was one of the main highways connecting the Midwest to Florida.

Then came the interstate, Interstate 75, which made the trip from Detroit to Miami fly by. It also made the tourists fly by. Once the interstate came, the business left—no more lines waiting to cross the Ohio River bridge. And with the interstate went one of the great distinctions in American business history. You see, before old Interstate 75,

From Florida with love.

the Kentucky Souvenir Shop in Milton, at the curve right before the bridge, was a tourist mecca. The tiny store sold more Florida souvenirs than any gift shop not in Florida.

A Kentucky gift shop located a souvenir ashtray's throw from the Ohio River sold more Florida souvenirs than any gift shop in America not in Florida? Sputter, choke, cough: How could that be? Simple. People would get to the river, a few hours from home, and remember what they forgot: to bring back a souvenir from Florida.

Kentucky Souvenir stocked up on stuffed alligators, pink flamingo ashtrays, and Florida window decals. And it did gangbuster business. Then they built the interstate, and that was it—no more tourists, no more Florida souvenirs flying out the door. Now it's just a simple little souvenir shop.

Kentucky Souvenir Shop is at 12921 US Highway 421 North. For information call (502) 268-3374.

Something Fishy
Newport

When most people think of Newport, they don't think of fish. Yeah, Newport is on the Ohio River, but the Ohio is not exactly a fisherman's paradise anymore. But Newport is home to one of the world's largest aquariums, what the advertising calls "one million gallons of fun." That's a lot of water.

Five local businessmen who love fish came up with the idea for an aquarium in 1990, but it took almost a decade to get the thing off the ground. (Well, it'll never be off the ground, not with a million gallons of water holding it down.) The aquarium finally opened in 1999 and it's one of the most popular attractions in northern Kentucky—second only to where George Clooney kissed his first girl.

The aquarium is home to 11,000 marine animals, including fifty sharks and twelve penguins. Penguins and sharks in Kentucky? You gotta see it to believe it.

★ ★

The aquarium is located on the Levee, a giant complex that includes retail stores and movie theaters, on Third Street, right on the Ohio River. For more information visit the website www.newportaquarium .com or call (859) 491-FINS (3467). FINS—that's cute.

Purple People Bridge
Newport

In 2001 the city of Newport, Kentucky, had the bright idea of purchasing a 123-year-old abandoned bridge over the Ohio River, thinking that local residents and tourists would pay $60 a head to climb the structure. Hah!

The city fathers projected that maybe 80,000 people a year would venture to the site, bringing in around $3 million annually. They even went so far as to give the bridge an identity by painting it purple, the Purple People Bridge, you know, playing off that old 1950's rock and roll hit, "Purple People Eater."

It turned out the bridge was a money-eater no matter the color. It never came close to meeting revenue projections and in 2007 the bridge climb closed.

But the bridge is still there and so is the $4 million debt for restoration. The bridge authority now sells certificates of ownership. Who doesn't want to own a piece of a purple bridge?

Today the bridge is used mainly for two things, walks and weddings. Your charity group can stage its fundraising walk and cross the Ohio. Or you can have your wedding on the bridge. The bridge averages a wedding a month. Really.

Who wouldn't want to get married on the largest pedestrian bridge in the US linking two states?

Actually you can rent it for just about any private event. Just contact Newport Southbank Bridge Company.

The Purple People Bridge is located at 421 Monmouth Street in Newport. For more information check out the website at www.purple peoplebridge.com.

★ ★

One Serious Bell
Newport

Ooo-eee, is this exciting. Pack up the kids, Mildred, we're heading to the world's largest free-swinging bell. Okay, it may not sound all that exciting, but this is one serious bell: thirty-three tons, twelve feet high, and twelve feet wide. It's the most serious bell since that original serious bell, the Liberty Bell.

Strike a note for world peace.

The World Peace Bell was built for the Millennium Moment, the turning of the twenty-first century. But it continues to ring loud and clear on special occasions, such as whenever its custodians decide to strike a note for world peace.

The bell is more than just a noisemaker; it's a sight. Its surface presents a sort of millennium's greatest hits: renderings of Columbus arriving in America, humans walking on the moon, Guttenberg creating moveable type, Einstein figuring out his Theory of Relativity. The inscription on the bell reads: "The World Peace Bell is a symbol of freedom and peace, honoring our past, celebrating our present, and inspiring our future."

And because the bell is pretty new—cast in 1998—there's no crack, like that bell in Philadelphia.

The World Peace Bell is at the corner of Fourth and York Streets. The World Peace Bell Center is located at 425 York Street, Newport.

Genesis Creation Museum

Petersburg

The sign on the door reads: "The Creation Museum is private property, a Christian environment, and an outreach of Answers in Genesis. Guests at the museum are expected to conduct themselves in a polite, respectful manner at all times. . . . Loud, disrespectful, disruptive, obscene or abusive behavior will not be tolerated, and any person engaging in such conduct or wearing clothing or items that are offensive to other guests or to our staff will be subject to removal from the premises."

The warning is warranted because when you walk in and see dinosaurs on Noah's Ark there's a good chance you might let out with a loud "Holy __!" or "What the hell?"

This state-of-the-art museum brings the pages of the Bible alive but also showcases historical accounts that are not mentioned in the Bible, such as dinosaurs and humans living side by side. The highlight of the *biblical history exhibit* is the scaffolding of Noah's Ark. The

★ ★

Mr. Noah, Mr. Dinosaur. . .

exhibit explains that dinosaurs were small enough to fit on Noah's Ark and that the Bible only explained 1 percent of the Noah's Ark story. Make sure you have plenty of time set aside for your visit; this exhibit alone takes two to three hours to complete. Be sure before leaving to visit the cinematic presentation of *Men In White*. This 3-D experience consists of two angels explaining life to inquisitive child Wendy through various biblical accounts and creative scientific reasoning. The museum also includes sections dedicated to the Scopes Monkey Trial and an area called Damnation Alley that details the heathenish ways of mankind.

And . . . and . . . you can visit some of the surviving animals of Noah's Ark at the outside petting zoo.

The Creation Museum is located at 2800 Bullittsburg Church Road in Petersburg. For more information check out the website at http://creationmuseum.org.

. . . Mr. Dinosaur, Mr. Noah.

★ ★

Down the Rabbit Hole to Rabbit Hash

Rabbit Hash

To get to the Rabbit Hash General Store, you have to want to get to the Rabbit Hash General Store. It's not on the way to anything; in fact they coined the expression "out of the way" just to describe its location. Step inside and it's like stepping back in time. But what would you expect from a store that's been open since 1831?

The swingingest place in town.

★ ★

Sometimes that time seems more like the '70s—the 1970s, not the 1870s. Ask for a candy bar, and you'll be offered an organic peanut butter cup. Ask for a soft drink, and you'll be directed to the Coke case, where you can purchase Coca-Cola in an old-fashioned six-ounce bottle—that is if you can get to the Coke case. There's often a dog sleeping in front of it. The store may be untouched by time, but the Ohio River hasn't been so kind. The place was submerged during the floods of 1884, 1913, and 1937. There's still mud from the '37 flood in the attic.

In addition to snack food, the store sells antiques, crafts, postcards, and my favorite item, the Rabbit Hash T-shirt, emblazoned with "Rabbit Hash Volunteer Fire Department, String Band, and S.W.A.T. Team."

Get off Interstate 75 at the Big Bone Lick State Park exit and head west. Stay on Highway 536; you'll find it. The website is www.rabbit hash.com.

Big Bone Lick State Park
Union

Hee-hee-hee, he said "Big Bone Lick." Fans of *Beavis and Butt-head* know what I'm talking about. The slightly risqué name for this state park often raises eyebrows. We have a number of sites in Kentucky that end in "lick"—and stir up the sophomore in all of us.

But Big Bone Lick is actually a very important area. Twelve thousand years ago, mammals pushed south by Ice Age glaciers found this site, with its mineral waters and salt lick. On any given prehistoric day you could find mastodons and mammoths, bison and ground sloths, shoulder to giant shoulder, basking in the swampy waters and licking the salt. Some became trapped in the marshes and died. Jump ahead to the 1700s, when early settlers discovered these *mammoth* mammoth bones and established the science of vertebrate paleontology.

The park celebrates its past with both an indoor and an outdoor museum, plus a diorama depicting its Ice Age glory. You can also camp, picnic, hike, and play miniature golf in the park.

Big Bone Lick State Park is at 3380 Beaver Road. For information call (859) 384-3522 or visit http://parks.ky.gov/parks/recreationparks/big-bone-lick/default.aspx.

Yeah, yeah, we know, it has a funny name.

Kentucky BBQ

We love barbecue in Kentucky, so much so that we stage festivals all over the state honoring this wondrous food. These barbecue festivals can make for a lively weekend outing. They're also a great place for tasting great barbecue.

At most festivals, once the judging is over the contestants start passing out free meat. All you have to do is stand in line. At others you may need to make friends. But that's easy enough. Barbecue cooks love to talk about their barbecue and their cooker.

You can find a barbecue festival somewhere just about every weekend during the summer.

Here are a few of the major ones.

May:	Bar-B-Q Festival Louisville's Pitt Academy, (502) 966-6979 Fountain Run Barbecue Festival Fountain Run, (270) 434-2915 International Bar-B-Q Festival Owensboro, (270) 926-6938
June:	W. C. Handy Blues & Barbecue Festival Henderson, (800) 648-3128 Microbrew and Bar-B-Q Festival Louisville's Churchill Downs, (502) 636-4400
July:	Bar-B-Que and Homecoming Dawson Springs, (270) 797-2781
September:	Barbecue on the River & Old Market Days Paducah, (270) 443-8783 or 800-PADUCAH
October:	Outdoor Expo and Barbecue Festival Madisonville, (270) 821-4171

★ ★

Eat Dessert First
Washington

Chocolate eggs. Hot chocolate. Chocolate bunnies. Chocolate pie.
Chocolate-covered cream candy. Chocolate cake. Chocolate chip cook-
ies. Bourbon balls. Turtles. Fudge. Bonbons. Toffee. Suckers. Chocolate

Quintessential Kentuckians
George Clooney

If more people had been interested in whole life insurance back in the
early 1980s, George Clooney's story would be in something called *The
Sample Case* instead of *Kentucky Curiosities.* But when George Clooney
was trolling the streets of Augusta, Kentucky, back then, dropping in
on people he didn't know during their dinnertime and trying to get
them interested in whole life insurance, well, as Clooney now says, "It
just didn't work."

After failing at selling life insurance—and, later, at selling shoes
and suits—Clooney took a job as a reporter on his mom's Cincinnati
cable TV show. In the summer of 1982 his cousin, actor Miguel Ferrer,
came to Lexington to make a movie about horses. George went down
to report on the movie and, while there, landed a small part. His film
work comprised one small scene in a movie that was never released.
But the bug had bitten.

George took $700 he earned cutting tobacco that fall and headed
to Los Angeles, crashing first at Aunt Rosey's house, then moving
in with a fellow actor. He worked construction by day and took acting lessons at night, living the life of the starving artist with small
roles in showcase performances and little theater plays. Soon he was

mousse. Chocolate pastry. Chocolate waffles. Chocolate ice cream.

Now that I have your attention, it's time to talk chocolate—and who doesn't want to talk about that subject? They've been celebrating that wonderful substance in Washington for more than a decade with the annual Chocolate Festival. Here you can walk through the old downtown sampling chocolate delights—now that's redundant—to your heart's

picking up supporting roles in TV pilots and series. But it was a string of near misses.

Beginning in the spring of '84 with a small part on the Elliott Gould comeback vehicle *E/R*, a CBS sitcom that was canceled before the season ended, he landed a succession of television roles that brought him money and familiarity but never stardom. He was in thirteen failed pilots and another seven series. (The low point of his career may have been the 1992 medical mystery *The Harvest*, which starred his cousin Miguel. George had a small role as a cross-dressing lambada teacher.)

Then came another *ER*, this one an NBC medical drama, and in 1994, at age thirty-three, George Clooney became a star. Soon he was on the cover of *People* magazine, touted as the Sexiest Man Alive. He left TV in 1999 to focus on his film career and in 2006 received the ultimate: three Oscar nominations for Best Supporting Actor, Best Director, and Best Screenplay—an achievement only two stars in Hollywood history had ever accomplished.

Despite the accolades, Clooney remains one of the most unassuming stars. When asked to speak at Career Day at his old high school, he pondered the honor. "What was I going to tell them? Quit college, move to L.A. and live with your rich aunt, and become an actor?"

He knows fame is fleeting, that someday his will go away. He has socked his money away. He told one interviewer, "I may end up in a trailer, but it will be a nice trailer."

★ ★

content on handmade candies, homemade cakes, handmade cook-
ies, homemade pies, handmade fudge. And while you are gorging on
all that sweet, delicious chocolate, you can feel good about yourself
because you are helping a worthy cause: Hospice of Southern Kentucky.

Washington is 1 mile south of the AA Highway on US Highway 68.
For information on the festival, held every March, call (606) 759-7423
or visit www.washingtonky.com/ChocFestPR.htm.

The Ghost of Spirits Past
Wilder

Most "ghost" sites are proud to claim one sighting. But Bobby Mackey's Music World is the mother of all haunted houses—some call it The
Most Haunted Place in America—with what must be a record twenty-
nine ghostly appearances, all backed up by affidavits.

It didn't start out that way. The original building was a slaughterhouse with a well in the basement for blood to drain. It was the lower
room that a satanic cult later chose for its regular rituals. On one occasion in 1896 that ritual allegedly involved the head of a Greencastle,
Indiana, woman, Pearl Bryan, who was killed by her boyfriend and
his pal after a botched abortion. The two were caught and convicted,
but, fearing the wrath of Satan, they would not disclose the location
of Pearl's missing head. On the gallows, the accused vowed he would
come back and get his revenge on the townspeople who had con-
demned him. Legend has it all the lawyers and judges involved in the
case died untimely deaths.

During Prohibition the slaughterhouse was razed and replaced by
a speakeasy, which eventually became a bar and casino known as
Buck Brady's Primrose. But it, too, came to an unhappy end after Red
Masterson, owner of the rival Merchant's Club, suggested that Brady
might want to sell out and Brady gave his answer with a double-
barreled shotgun. No charges were filed against Brady; Masterson lived
but claimed he couldn't identify his assailant. But something trans-
pired, because soon Brady sold out to the Cleveland syndicate, which

A bar popular for its spirits.

renamed the place the Latin Quarter. Sometime before the Quarter was shut down in the early 1960s after a gambling raid, a club manager's daughter named Johanna committed suicide in the basement.

In 1970 the place morphed into a roadhouse called Hard Rock Cafe (no relation to the chain), which was shut down in 1978 after a series of fatal shootings. That's when Bobby and Janet Mackey purchased the building and turned it into a country music bar popular for its spirits of the alcoholic variety. In the past two decades there have been reports of scary sounds, spooky sightings of a headless ghost (that would be Pearl Ryan), apparitions of angry men (probably her killers), and a spirit calling herself "Johanna."

Writer Doug Hensley has put this story together in great detail in his book *Hell's Gate*. Read it and you will believe.

Bobby Mackey's Music World is located at 44 Licking Pike in Wilder. The website is www.bobbymackey.com/hellsgate.html.

Quintessential Kentuckians

Adolph Rupp, The Baron of The Bluegrass

The Baron of The Bluegrass wasn't born in The Bluegrass. He was born in Halstead, Kansas, in 1901 and graduated from Kansas University. But Adolph Rupp is forever linked to Kentucky because he put Kentucky on the map. During his forty-two years as head coach of the University of Kentucky basketball team, 1930 to 1972, he won 876 games, 4 national championships, and 27 conference championships—and made Kentucky a household word during basketball season.

How did he do it? In a word: desire. Rupp had a competitive streak rivaled by none. He famously said, "I know I have plenty of enemies, but I'd rather be the most hated winning coach in the country than the most popular losing one." Even his players disliked him.

And opposing teams? They were his mortal enemies. During a game in the late 1940s—a time when Rupp won three national titles—his team held a halftime lead of 38–4 over an out-manned team, and still Rupp was raging. It seems all four of the opponent's points had been scored by a single player. Rupp wanted him stopped. "Somebody guard that man. Why, he's running wild!"

In 1951 Rupp was asked to compare his current team, which would go on to win the NCAA championship, to his '47–'48 team, which had also won a national title. He responded in typical Rupp fashion. "They [the '48 team] liked to crush everybody early and get it over with. This bunch is tender-hearted—the only one they're killing is me."

Rupp's record of career wins was surpassed in 1997 by University of North Carolina coach Dean Smith, who had the advantage of coaching in an era when teams played more games per season. Had Rupp known that some other coach might surpass his record, he most assuredly would have died on the sideline.

index

index

index

index

index

index

index

about the author

Vince Staten is the author of thirteen books, including the bestsellers *Did Monkeys Invent the Monkey Wrench?* and *Jack Daniel's Old-Time Barbecue Cookbook.* He is a freelance writer, author, syndicated columnist, movie critic, lecturer, professor and restaurateur. (And one of these days he plans to settle down and pick a career.) His writings have appeared in many newspapers, including the *New York Times, Boston Globe, Dallas Times Herald, Baltimore Sun,* and Kingsport, Tennessee *Times-News,* and *Review, Icon,* and *Bon Appetit* magazines. For seven years he served as a Commissioner of the City of River Bluff, Kentucky (population 356). He was never indicted.